DAILY LIFE IN HITLER'S
GERMANY

DAILY LIFE IN HITLER'S
GERMANY

Dr. Matthew Seligmann
Dr. John Davison
John McDonald

THOMAS DUNNE BOOKS

St. Martin's Press
New York

Copyright © 2003 The Brown Reference Group plc

ISBN 0-312-32811-7

First published in the US in 2004 by
THOMAS DUNNE BOOKS
An imprint of St. Martin's Press,
175 Fifth Avenue, New York, N.Y.10010
www.stmartins.com

1 3 5 7 9 8 6 4 2

Editorial and Design:
The Brown Reference Group plc
8 Chapel Place
Rivington Street
London
EC2A 3DQ

Senior Editor: Peter Darman
Editor: Alan Marshall
Picture Researcher: Andrew Webb
Designer: Anthony Cohen
Production Director: Alastair Gourlay

Printed in China

Contents

Introduction
How Nazi Germany came into being

There was nothing inevitable about the NSDAP becoming the ruling party in Germany; indeed, during the 1920s the Nazis experienced a series of electoral reverses. However, a series of economic and political factors combined to propel Hitler into power.

There was nothing inevitable about the rise to power of Adolf Hitler and the Nazi Party. In fact, there was little in the history of Germany's National Socialist movement to suggest that its followers were marked out for high office. During much of the 1920s, the National Socialist German Workers' Party (NSDAP) was little more than a small and disreputable fringe, right-wing, extremist organization with limited popular appeal. Its leader was an undistinguished Austrian dilettante, who had failed to get into art school in Vienna and whose principal claim to fame was his criminal conviction for launching a bungled attempt to overthrow the state, in November 1923 – the so-called "Beer Hall *Putsch*". All of this placed the Nazis firmly on the margin of mainstream

Below: Adolf Hitler (centre of picture), Nazi leader, at a party rally in Nuremberg in January 1923. To Hitler's left, with a bald head, stands the rabid anti-Semite Julius Streicher.

Above: Hitler (seated, in centre) talks with Franz von Papen (seated, right) on the day the Nazi Party leader became Chancellor of Germany – 30 January 1933. To Hitler's right sits Hermann Göring.

politics. Throughout the 1920s, for example, they received a tiny proportion of the electoral vote: 6.6 percent in May 1924; just three percent in December of the same year; and then a meagre 2.6 percent in May 1928. Even at their peak in May 1924, they won only 32 out of the 472 seats in Germany's parliament, the *Reichstag*. This total tumbled to 14 and then 12 in subsequent elections. In spite of this dismal record, Hitler became Chancellor of the German Reich in January 1933. How did this come about?

German politics underwent a transformation in the wake of the economic collapse that followed the Wall Street crash of October 1929. As the German economy headed for disaster, millions of workers were pushed into unemployment and their families became destitute. The reputations of the mainstream political parties responsible for governing Germany went into a nose-dive. Those parties that had never been part of government and were untainted by association with Germany's economic malaise began to gain support. Voters who would never previously have considered extremist organizations decided to trust parties that held the view that desperate times required radical solutions. One such group was the Nazi Party, and the result was a massive increase in its vote. From 810,000 votes in 1928, the Nazis polled a staggering 6.4 million in 1930. Suddenly the party had 107 seats in the *Reichstag*, a total that rose to 230 in the July 1932 elections when 13.7 million people cast their vote for the NSDAP.

Dramatic though its effects were, the Wall Street crash alone cannot explain Hitler's rise to power. The electoral successes described above could not in themselves put the Nazis into government. The 230 seats they won represented only 37.3 percent of the vote, a long way from a working majority in the *Reichstag*. It was just at this juncture that the worst of the

recession began to abate and the electoral fortunes of the Nazis started to slump. Three months later, in the November 1932 elections, the party lost two million votes and was reduced to 196 seats. Observing this decline, many contemporary commentators believed that the Nazi Party's prominence was over and that its success would prove to have been a temporary phenomenon. It was at this point, though, that a second factor came into play.

This was the political strategy adopted by the other right-wing parties and their leaders. Particularly important were the activities and machinations of Franz von Papen. A notoriously inept and profoundly foolish Catholic nobleman, von Papen had achieved notoriety during World War I when, as German military attaché to Washington DC, he had been expelled from the US on grounds of passport fraud and sabotage. Having helped undermine Germany overseas, von Papen next turned his attention to ruining the country at home. Appointed Chancellor in 1932, he presided over an administration that was both ineffectual and short-lived. Somehow, despite this record of consistent and monumental failure, von Papen managed to gain the ear of the elderly German President, Paul von Hindenburg. Mustering all the poor judgement at his disposal, von Papen decided to use this influence to shape German politics by having Hitler appointed as chancellor. This was no easy task. Throughout 1932, von Hindenburg, who despised Hitler, had steadfastly refused to appoint to the chancellorship the man he disparagingly called "the Bohemian Corporal". Unfortunately, von Papen was able to persuade the President to go against his better judgement. He argued that the Nazis needed to be brought into government. Their 196 *Reichstag* seats, he told von Hindenburg, could be used to give the German right a real majority in parliament and thus a real grip on power. He convinced the President that, as part of a coalition government, the Nazis could be kept under control. The other right-wing parties, he maintained, would dominate the government. In the face of this argument Hindenburg gave in, with the result that, in January 1933, Hitler was sworn in as Chancellor of a coalition right-wing government.

Once in office, Hitler quickly shattered all of von Papen's assertions about the other parties' ability to control the Nazis. Although there were only three Nazis in the new coalition cabinet – Hitler, Hermann Göring and Wilhelm Frick – this proved sufficient for a National Socialist takeover. Particularly important was the fact that, in the new government, the Nazis controlled the Reich Interior Ministry as well as the Interior Ministry of Prussia, the largest German state. This gave them power over the police, a power that was used to persecute the Nazis' enemies and to legalize street terror and intimidation by Hitler's private army, the *Sturmabteilung* (SA, or stormtroopers). By such means, the parties of the left were effectively

forced off the streets and out of existence. Subsequently, by ensuring the passage of an enabling law through a now subservient parliament, Hitler obtained the power to rule by decree. Having done this, the Nazi leader was then able to dispense with his erstwhile allies. In July 1933, a mere six months after he had been appointed Chancellor, Hitler had all parties other than the NSDAP banned. From then on, Germany was living in the shadow of the swastika. Just what this meant for the German people will be explored in the next 12 chapters.

Above: Members of the Nazi paramilitary SA organization. SA members, who numbered two million in 1933, fought leftists and generally intimidated voters in national and local elections.

Left: Wilhelm Frick, Hitler's minister of the interior, was first elected to the *Reichstag* in May 1924. He served in his post until 1943, when he was replaced by Himmler. Tried at Nuremberg after World War II, Frick was hanged in 1946.

Chapter 1
The Nazi police state

In their quest to establish a "People's Community", the Nazis used the law and the police to crush all forms of opposition. The result was a police state in which arbitrary arrest and state brutality ensured that the population remained subservient.

George Orwell's famous description of fascism as a boot stamping again and again on a human face is a vivid and chilling image, but is it a reliable representation of the reality of the police state created in Germany after 1933?

Certainly in the turmoil of the early months after the so-called seizure of power in January 1933 Nazi activists in the *Sturmabteilung*, or brown-shirted stormtroopers (hereafter SA), especially acted violently, without fear of the law being used against them by the government. Georg Glaser, a novelist, recollected that after Hitler was named Chancellor, "dead bodies were found in the surrounding forests and no one dared to know anything about them. People disappeared without a sound, and their best friends did not have the courage to ask where they had gone. Only rarely did a scream, a gruesome rumour ... make itself heard; they were paid less notice than everyday traffic incidents."

These Nazi attacks cost 80 members of the old *Reichstag* (parliament) their lives; another 160 were exiled, including two former chancellors, Josef Wirth and

Left: The interior of the *Reichstag* after the arson attack of 27 February 1933. The fire was used by the Nazis to usher in emergency powers, such as the Decree of the President for the Protection of the People and the State.

Heinrich Brünning, who fled from Germany. Another, General Schleicher, remained and was later murdered. With the *Reichstag* Fire in February 1933, the Nazis in government were to initiate legislation that would eventually stifle all true freedoms. The first step in the artificially whipped-up frenzy after the fire was the Decree of the President for the Protection of the People and the State (28 February 1933), which finally abolished rights that the Weimar constitution had guaranteed, even if in the period of creeping authoritarianism from 1930 to 1933 those rights had been ignored. This decree ended freedom of assembly and expression – it also authorized the arbitrary opening of letters in the post, telephone tapping and allowed searches and indefinite detention without the necessity of a warrant.

In this legitimized emergency the arbitrary arrests by police, the SA or emerging SS groups (*Schutz Staffel*, or Protection Division) were less about maintaining law and order than dealing with political opposition, particularly the communists, who were so hated by the Nazis. It was an opportunity for the new masters to settle scores and seek revenge against whomsoever they selected, venting their spite on Jehovah's Witnesses, as well as socialists, Catholics and communists.

The emerging police state

This was the beginning in chaotic form of what was gradually to be formalized and institutionalized into a Nazi police state. Arbitrary police terror, as the author Michael Burleigh has recently argued,

overrode the rule of law to such an extent that in reality this was "the crucial breach with the most fundamental characteristic of free societies", a breach with civilized values, out of which subsequent Nazi atrocities, both in peace and war, were to develop.

So, two particular questions emerge, which are the focus of this chapter: in what ways was the rule of

Left: With the coming to power of the Nazis the persecution of the Jews intensified. Here, in Cuxhaven, a woman is ridiculed and made to wear a placard by SA men because of her relationship with a Jewish man.

Below: Members of the SS during a training exercise. Originally formed in 1925 as a small bodyguard to protect Hitler, by 1933 it numbered 52,000. The SS was the Nazi Party's racial and ideological élite.

law bypassed; and what were the agencies for enforcing the emerging Nazi terror?

The law overridden

Initially, on coming to office, the Nazis did not envisage comprehensive law reform nor a new legal code. For that would confine those who wished to exercise their new power and authority without restrictions. Following Hitler's principle that he should be able to fulfil his will, legal codes were deemed inappropriate; instead, existing laws were subverted and new decrees were issued to legitimize whatever actions were desired. In extreme cases even the decrees were brought in and applied retrospectively to justify illegal actions that had already been carried out. A good example of this was that by the decree of 3 July 1934, Hitler legitimized the murders of the SA leadership and other victims of the Night of the Long Knives (30 June 1934), which he had ordered earlier.

Hitler and his party sought to realize aims of racial purity, national coordination and the creation of the *Volksgemeinschaft* (People's Community). These aims were undeniably utopian, that is to create a perfect world. Therefore, the idea that they should be prevented by the technicalities of outdated laws from realizing their goals was unthinkable. Hitler's will, as it emerged in policies, had to prevail. The desire to achieve goals despite the law was revealed in many harsh and coercive decrees. Between 1933 and 1939, offences punishable by death increased from 3 to over 40. Crimes which Hitler personally detested were quickly added to the list, child kidnapping for one and for anybody who used roadblocks while robbing drivers on the prestigious new *Autobahnen* (motorways). But it was not merely an increase in capital offences that occurred, but also in actual executions. In the Weimar Republic from 1919 to 1932, some 1141 people were sentenced to death and 184 executed. Under the Nazis from 1933 to 1939, more than 80 percent of those convicted of capital offences

„Immer vornehm!" Flottenmeuterer "Bernh. Kuhnt fährt an seiner neuen Arbeitsstätte (Dreckwaschen) vor.

(records of the exact numbers no longer survive) were executed. The usual distinction between judiciary (law courts) and executive functions (government) was ended, and ultimately some presumed common good of the People's Community was proclaimed to be superior to individual rights – particularly if that individual was deemed to be racially inferior (a Jew or a gypsy) or belonged to a stigmatized group (the anti-social, homosexual or work-shy), or those deemed on health and psychological grounds to be unworthy of membership of that national community.

A 1933 law against "Dangerous Habitual Criminals" allowed for the sentence to be followed on its completion by the detention of the offender if classified as a permanent danger to that mythical *Volksgemeinschaft*. This extract from a circular sent out by *Gestapo* chief Heinrich Müller, dated 5 August 1937, to *Gestapo* offices illustrates this point:

Protective custody for Jehovah's Witnesses:

If information regarding the impending release of a Jehovah's Witness from arrest is received ... transfer to a concentration camp can take place immediately after the sentence has been served. If it is impossible to transfer Jehovah's Witnesses to a concentration camp immediately after the securing of the sentence, they will be retained in prison.

Given that there were judges and courts, which carried over from earlier, more liberal times, one way of subverting these restraints was to create special courts to deal with special emergencies – and given Hitler's and the regime's preoccupations with Darwinian (that in human society the strong invariably grow in power and in cultural influence over the weak – the "survival of the fittest") struggles and images of war – emergencies were always claimed to exist. By 1938 more than 70 such special courts had been created, many of which sought to enforce uniformity of outlook by persecuting those foolish enough to gossip or be indiscreet enough to speak out. Being drunk was no

Above: As well as the Jews, the communists were also a target in the early days of Nazi Germany. This scene from Chemnitz shows a local communist being taken away by SA and SS men.

excuse, as a Düsseldorf docker who spoke of Hitler as "a prole" and "sack of shit" was to learn when he received an 18-month sentence.

Police enforcement

The abiding image of the Nazi regime as a repressive police state is personified in the black-shirted SS man. From their later dominant position it is hard to recognize this image of terror in the tiny groups of men who, in 1925, created the original SS formed out of the larger SA. In 1929 Heinrich Himmler became *Reichsführer-SS*, or SS National Leader, and transformed the organization from a group of 280 men to no fewer than 52,000 at Hitler's takeover in 1933. By the outbreak of war in 1939 they numbered 250,000. Despite its numerical growth it was seen as an élite group, whose pedigrees were vetted back to the eighteenth century. Their racial background was investigated to ensure that no Jewish relatives existed; and Himmler was equally intrusive into racial lineage in his concern with future marriage

Left: Enforcers of the one-party state (from right to left): Ernst Röhm, head of the SA; Heinrich Himmler, head of the SS; and Kurt Daluege, who in 1933 was given control of the German police.

partners for his élite. Himmler, as their leader, was obsessively preoccupied with their ideological correctness, too. When, in 1939, he became Reich Commissioner for the Strengthening of German Nationhood, this ensured that his SS organization was central to the direction and implementation of Nazi

Below: The police state in action: a member of the *Gestapo* (centre, holding papers), conducts a spot-check of identity papers in front of a cafe in Berlin in early 1938.

racial and population policy in Eastern Europe, culminating in the Final Solution (mass murder of the Jews, see Chapter 9).

Within the SS another agency was created, the SD (*Sicherheitsdienst*, or Security Service), which acted as a party secret service concerned with combating the Nazis' enemies. After 1934, with the Nazis in charge of a one-party state, this became the agency to control all the party's intelligence services. Under the leadership of Reinhard Heydrich, it also saw itself as the true intellectual and ideological core of the Nazi movement: its think-tank.

The police forces

Besides these two bodies, German police forces (the so-called "ordinary police") before 1933 were decentralized, each force being under the control of its respective *Länder* – county or state authority – for example, Bavaria in the south, Prussia in the north. One of the most remarkable aspects of the police state as it emerged is that the bulk of ordinary policemen kept their jobs and did not find it hard to adjust to the new regime and its "law and order" policies. Hitler received reports in 1934 showing that 98 percent of Prussia's uniformed police and more than 90 percent of its officers were to be allowed to stay on. Similarly, the detectives in the criminal police (*Kripo*, part of the SS) were little affected, with more than 11,500 across the Reich keeping their jobs. If the number of detectives in the *Kripo* was reduced between 1933 and 1935, it was because they were transferred to the *Gestapo* (State Secret Police in Prussia) where their professional skills were sought – more of a promotion than a purge. One can only conclude that most policemen were content to participate in a regime that not only claimed to be fighting crime but seemed to be

Left: Gregor Strasser, a leading Nazi who was murdered during the Night of the Long Knives in June 1934. To justify such illegal actions, decrees were brought in by the Nazis and applied retrospectively.

giving the police the scope to act as they saw fit.

Having at first been made head of Bavaria's police, Heinrich Himmler in 1934 was placed in charge of the *Gestapo*. This range of jobs was added to in June 1936 when Hitler appointed him head of all the nation's police services with the obvious task of making them Nazified. The expected reorganization came in 1938 with the creation of the RSHA (*Reichssicherheitshauptamt*, Reich

15

Security Head Office), and was finalized in 1939. Hitler now had overall control of all police and security forces in Germany.

So there now existed one overall police authority directly under Himmler (and ultimately Hitler) beyond the control of any other agency, with the implication that the security of the state and the security of the party were not separate activities. This meant that an SS man might in one context operate as what seemed like a traditional policeman. As such he would perhaps merit the normal and conventional citizen's respect and deference. In another context, the same SS man would be a completely unregulated agent of Himmler's (or the Führer's) wishes; acting outside the law in a way that evoked terror and fear. These SS men took a special binding oath, not to Germany, but to Hitler alone:

We swear to you Adolf Hitler, as Führer and Chancellor of the German Reich, to be loyal and brave. We vow to you and the superiors appointed by you obedience unto death. So help us God.

Thus Hitler had an instrument of force, which could act completely outside all the restraints of the traditional government framework – as it was to do so increasingly in Germany and more especially in the war-conquered territories after 1939.

The concentration camps
One particular and characteristic function of the SS was to be placed in charge of Germany's new and Nazi-created system of concentration camps. The first was established in the suburb of Dachau in March 1933. The first victims or inmates of the brutal regime imprisoned there were the Nazis' political enemies, principally communists and socialists. Arrests of approximately 25,000 people in Prussia alone in March and

April 1933 are officially reported in police records, and these do not include those "wild arrests" of political opponents made by the SA and the SS. By 31 July 1933, 26,789 prisoners were held in protective custody in the Reich. By March 1935, in the concentration camps centred on Dachau, there were between 7000 to 9000 prisoners (low by later standards). But these numbers could arbitrarily be extended, as on the morning of 10 November 1938 when, following *Kristallnacht* (a nation-wide attack on Jewish property and synagogues), 30,000 healthy male Jews were ordered to be arrested by Heydrich (Himmler's deputy), of whom 200 or so were to die. A report said: "the events of the last few days have increased the number of

Above: Black-uniformed members of the *Leibstandarte*, Hitler's bodyguard. All members of the SS swore a personal oath of loyalty to Hitler alone, thus making them unregulated agents of the Führer.

prisoners from 24,000 (in camps) to roughly 60,000." Many were to be short-term prisoners, for as the figures reveal, at the outbreak of war in September 1939 there were roughly 25,000 prisoners. These numbers would be dwarfed by the war years and the vast increase in camp populations.

Yet, as the camp network expanded to Sachsenhausen (1936), Buchenwald (1937) and Flossenbürg (1938), the number and range of prisoners was ever greater. Also created in 1938 was Mauthausen, whose purpose was to deal with a fresh wave of political and racial enemies in the newly incorporated Austria. Here the camp was based in a stone and marble quarry, where the SS used the prisoners for virtual slave labour to hew the raw material for Hitler's grandiose rebuilding of Germany's cities in a manner befitting a Thousand Year Reich. Hitler frequently looked over the plans and models of a rebuilt Linz (his home town) as the emaciated prisoners worked themselves to death. Their blood swelled the coffers of the SS building enterprises' income from the sale of the marble to state agencies.

Life in the camps

These camps became a byword for brutality and arbitrary violence inflicted on prisoners. Whatever weasel and self-hypocritical words their commandants or their ultimate boss, Himmler, might utter – "the concentration camp is certainly a harsh and tough measure," he said in 1939 – they were designed to both isolate and destroy the power of the prisoners. The regimes were simply licensed brutality in a totally controlled context.

Prisoners on arrival could expect all their possessions to be taken, their heads shaved and they would be given a number. Depersonalization went

further as they were treated as categories not people – criminal, gypsy, political, homosexual, Jehovah's Witness, anti-social, Jew – and they were colour coded accordingly.

The regime consisted of both purposeful activity (quarrying) and purposeless activities, which wore down still further the exhausted and malnourished prisoners. Added to this was a constant diet of fear induced by random roll calls,

Above: An early photograph of Sachsenhausen concentration camp, 34km (21 miles) northwest of Berlin. Of the 200,000 prisoners who passed through the camp, 100,000 died from disease, executions, and overwork.

arbitrary brutality from guards, beatings and shootings, as well as sadistic games from their captors. The Mauthausen prisoners were called "parachutists" by their guards, who threw them off the edge of the quarry for reasons only their sick psyches could explain.

Incarceration in the camps impacted not only on prisoners, of course, but also on their families and friends. Frau Winklehner, for example, was informed of her husband's death in Dachau and with a friend drove to the camp to view the body:

The next morning at 6 o'clock we were at the camp gate and begged admittance. Our identification was taken, then we were locked in a waiting room. From there we saw the inmates fall in for morning roll call. Later we saw how they marched out to work. We had to wait four hours. We went across the parade ground to a tiny house. The door was opened. On a pedestal stood a coffin; Herr Winklehner, embedded in sawdust and with his mouth open, lay inside. Frau Winklehner wanted to caress him. "Hands off!" screamed the SS man. [We] asked what he died of. "Disturbance of the circulation – visit ended," came the short and concise reply.

Like the more regular prison system alongside which these camps existed, a prisoner's release (always assuming he or she survived) was usually conditional. Infractions included giving false (that is, true) information about their experiences, which could result in re-arrest and so-called "protective custody".

Information about these camps was hard to come by for German citizens. Rumours abounded, aided by adverse criticism in the foreign press and media, but the Nazi Government also fed information into local and

Above: A roll call of inmates in Sachsenhausen concentration camp in 1936. Note the triangles on the uniforms. These depicted categories of prisoners, i.e. homosexual, anti-social or political.

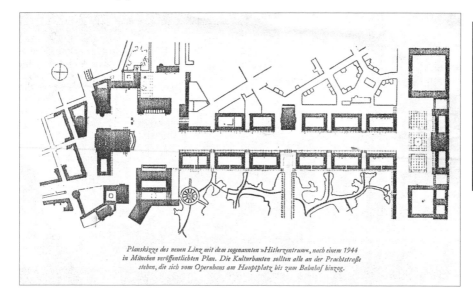

Planskizze des neuen Linz mit dem sogenannten »Hitlerzentrum«, nach einem 1944 in München veröffentlichten Plan. Die Kulturbauten sollten alle an der Prachtstraße stehen, die sich vom Opernhaus am Hauptplatz bis zum Bahnhof hinzog.

Left: Hitler's plan for the rebuilding of Linz (his home town), Austria. The materials for such projects were often produced by concentration camp inmates, who were worked to death by their SS masters.

regional newspapers, issued reports and showed highly sanitized photographs and films of "real" conditions in the camps. But the German public were sufficiently aware of the less rosy version of these camps for them to be thought of as a suitable punishment; for those who were in them clearly deserved to be there. They were also to act as a deterrent for any would-be critics: Germany's citizens were deprived of the freedom to speak freely, an inescapable feature of the police state in which they lived.

Everything presented so far has shown a growing number of police organizations showing a generalized disregard for individual rights, as they sought to coerce and cower the German population. This is a classic image of a dictatorial system and a police state.

Support for the Nazis

However, there have been those who have argued, and principally among them is the Canadian historian Robert Gellately, that the extent of terror and coercion has been overstated. In his writings about the *Gestapo* and more recently in his book *Backing Hitler*, Gellately has stressed the degree of popular support that the regime enjoyed on the back of mounting economic progress and a declining unemployment rate, coupled with increasing success in the international field as the Nazi Government freed itself from the constraints of the Treaty of Versailles, the peace settlement that ended World War I. The Nazis reintroduced conscription and developed an air force and navy. These paved the way for remilitarization of the Rhineland in 1936 and the *Anschluss* (Union) with Austria in March 1938 – all before a further wave of military victories in 1939 and 1940 raised nationalist fervour to a crescendo. By stressing

the degree of popularity enjoyed by Hitler and the Nazi regime, Gellately emphasizes the level of consent present in Germany for the government, which had come to power in a constitutional way, even if many of its subsequent actions were harsh and violent, and illegal. Gellately suggests that most people accepted as normal a tough regime with harsh punishments. One striking

Above: Inmates of Sachsenhausen concentration camp breaking up clay for the brickworks. All inmates had to work; those unable to work died of starvation. Even those who did not starve often died from overwork.

19

measure of the consent, he claims, is the extent of denunciations by ordinary citizens of their neighbours to the *Gestapo*.

The *Gestapo*

Gestapo agents were far more thinly spread on the ground than their mythical omnipresence (reputation for being everywhere) would suggest. He claims only some 32,000 for the whole of Germany in 1944. The *Gestapo*, he suggests, were significantly reliant on denunciations to be able to keep such an extensive watch over nearly 80 million people. While ideological enthusiasm may have prompted some denunciations, others were more personally and vindictively motivated by neighbours and acquaintances, who wrote to the *Gestapo* to complain of a neighbour's sexual behaviour (alleged lesbianism), Jewishness or sympathies with Jews. As Gellately points out: "It was a characteristic feature of the Third Reich ... that the regime found no difficulty in obtaining the collaboration of ordinary citizens."

Not only was this willingness to cooperate and denounce to have a devastating effect on German resistance (see Chapter 3), but in more general terms it was essential to help the Nazis realize their ideological aims and made dictatorship work. While this argument by Gellately is a useful corrective to oversimplifications about dictatorships or terror, it does exaggerate the level of complicity when most Germans were not necessarily active zealots for the regime, nor yet resistors. Instead, the majority were probably pursuing the almost unavoidable path of accommodation: in the search for jobs, food, housing, marriage partners and a more secure future in a society where there were no opposition parties, nor any forum for expressing dissatisfaction. The only public opinion was official Nazi views, which informed the populace about concentration camps and preventative detention. Only the recklessly brave or irredeemably foolhardy would do other than keep their heads down, and their noses apparently clean! So, it is easy to exaggerate the degree of consent and underestimate the degree of self-

Below: German forces parade through Vienna during the *Anschluss* with Austria in March 1938. The peaceful union with a German-speaking nation was very popular throughout the Reich.

preservation that a German citizen showed. Repression and threat were always there, and they worked.

Another more personal and direct sense of being in a police state exists in the recorded experiences of German citizens. Bernt Engelmann, from Düsseldorf, describes how he learnt about torture from Hedwig, a former servant of his family. Her husband Fritz had been arrested by the *Gestapo* two weeks earlier just as he was leaving for work:

First they squeezed him into an iron locker. He was jammed in there for 12 hours until late in the evening. Then they came back and interrogated him. First they drove little pointed sticks under his nails .... As she continued I felt so sick ... that I had to run to the lavatory. After this, Hedwig came to see us often. One time she had just received a letter from her husband, who was now in a concentration camp in Emsland. He wrote that he was all right, considering the circumstances. My mother promptly made up a parcel for him that Hedwig was to mail ... A year later Fritz was released. He even found a job again and on one of the first Sundays after his return he came by just to say hello and thanks. Since we knew that former concentration camp inmates were not allowed to speak about their experiences we did not press him. "Did you notice," my mother asked just after he had left, "that his hair had turned completely grey?"

Two German citizens who at different times suffered arbitrary arrests and who kept immediate records of their experiences were Victor Klemperer and Luise Rinser. Both prisoners survived the Nazi period and their prison writings were subsequently published.

Victor Klemperer, a German university professor from Dresden, kept diaries from 1933 to 1945, in which he records in great detail his

daily thoughts and experiences throughout the Nazi period (see Chapter 12). In 1941, he was arrested for carelessly and inadvertently not drawing a black-out curtain over a window – he was denounced by a neighbour and placed in custody for eight days. Using the prison pencil he was issued with he kept notes on his experiences, and on his release wrote them up in his diary where they span some 25 pages. Here are some of his experiences from Cell 89 from 23 June to 1 July 1941:

Top: German artillery passes through the streets of Cologne in the 1930s. Conscription and rearmament made the Nazis very popular among ordinary Germans.
Above: An SS officer hands out cigarettes to concentration camp inmates in this propaganda shot from the 1930s.

Nowhere, nowhere even among the Jews, was there a known case of imprisonment for a first time black-out misdemeanour; the usual fine was now said to amount to 50 M [marks], possibly they would make it far more for non-Aryans; money was needed, the prisons were overcrowded. My petition was rejected.

I felt very bitter, for I undoubtedly owed it solely to the J on my identity card. Police custody was not imprisonment, the police were not brutal like the Gestapo. *How could I know beforehand, what imprisonment, what a cell is? Only at the second that the door fell shut, did I know it with a nameless fear. At that second eight days turned into 192 hours – empty, caged hours.*

Since his imprisonment coincided with the German invasion of the Soviet Union, when some military patriotic music filtered into his cell, he thought: "All at once I was afraid the final victory could be Hitler's and with it his permanent rule." But, finally, he was released: "My wife was waiting."

The second, more threatening account is from the experiences of Luise Rinser, who was born in 1911 in Bavaria. A widow with two children, she was a writer whose first novel was published the same year as Klemperer's imprisonment. She had fallen under suspicion and the *Gestapo* were keeping surveillance on her when, in 1944, she was denounced by a woman she had considered to be a friend. This denunciation led to a charge of high treason and she faced a death sentence, which only the defeat of Germany prevented. While in prison awaiting sentence she kept a journal, which was first published after the war in 1946. As she said then:

I am publishing my prison journal. I am not doing this because my personal fate seems important to me. It is merely one among many thousands. But because it is one among thousands, *it is possible for me to publish this book. It does not speak of anything extraordinary, anything that might match the sufferings of those who were in concentration camps.*

Arrested in 1944, she wrote on 3 November 1944:

Since yesterday I have no longer been in my solitary cell but in with four others. Being together with others like this has one advantage; at difficult times you don't feel so lonely. Everything else is a

Above: The individual had no defence against state Nazi terror – a communist is assaulted by SA men.

Below: The kitchens at Dachau. Even petty denunciations could result in incarceration in a concentration camp.

disadvantage ... at night they use the bucket 4 or 5 times, very noisily, one of them has diarrhoea, another stinks, one wants the window open at night, another has rheumatism and wants it shut. There is still no heating. Outside there is already snow ... At night I can scarcely sleep for the cold. My cough and my kidney pain are unbearable.

Why was she there? She had initially given cigarettes to Russian prisoners of war.

Repression increases

These two relatively mild and unsensational accounts of prison as experienced by two citizens of education, respectability and responsibility are not representative of the extremities to which the system descended. Yet they show how innocent citizens could be swept up and criminalized by a regime where no control was exercised over the police state, and where the police recognized no limits on their powers and actions. The full extent to which this could descend was demonstrated in the Final Solution. The death camps created by the SS in Poland are not to be confused with the concentration camps discussed in this chapter. They are, however, a logical outcome to the brutality that the Nazi police state inflicted on its own citizens. This violence and brutality increased in the final years of the war when the prospect of defeat led the regime to turn ever more viciously on its citizens. Whereas the early years of the war perhaps added a patriotic layer of cohesion to the state; later, especially after the defeat at Stalingrad in early 1943, the more repressive face of the police state revealed itself again.

This might have partly been in response to continued denunciations by citizens, no matter how petty. For example, Gertrude Schulz, a 48-year-old married woman, denounced her landlord on 10 November 1943. She had been his tenant since 1938, but he objected to the chickens she and her husband kept. She exaggerated and added to the negative remarks about Hitler that the landlord had made. By February 1944 the landlord was handed over to the *Gestapo* and sent to Berlin, where he was found guilty by the People's Court –

Below: The archetypal Nazi family. Rather than being rabid National Socialists, most Germans tried to provide for their families and stay out of trouble.

Above: German troops on the march. As the war continued and German defeat appeared inevitable, the army, along with the SS, became increasingly involved in the enforcement of Nazi dictates.

Left: At times of national emergencies the army would be called upon to enforce the Führer's will. This often meant mass arrests and executions. Here, German soldiers stand guard in Berlin in the aftermath of the June 1934 Night of the Long Knives.

founded in 1934 – sentenced to death and executed on 17 July 1944.

Despite the particularly deadly outcome to this case, the situation was to worsen. Increasingly in the last six months of the war, with conflict moving into Germany itself, reprisals and shootings of citizens became widespread. People who were thought to be wavering in the required belief in Germany's ultimate victory, or raised questions about the value of Germany continuing the war, were to be dealt with. On 15 February 1945, Hitler created the Drum-Head Courts, each one usually comprised of a Nazi Party official and a *Wehrmacht* (army) officer, or one from the SS or the police. Such a court would try anyone thought to be a danger to the Nazi cause or not wholly committed to the war effort. As a consequence, rough and ready trials followed by executions were widespread. These trials were filled with emotions of revenge, bitterness and fear.

So, in its dying throes the Nazi police state turned on its helpless citizens once again. In angry violence the citizens were to be punished by the state for their alleged failure to live up to the role and utopian ideals that the Nazi police state had imposed on them. As in 1933, so in 1945, the regime considered its citizens only as part of a community apparently still filled with categories of deficient people who had to be punished or destroyed. So the Nazi boot, as Orwell might have said, hit the face again and again.

Above: Prisoners about to be executed following their conviction by a Drum Head Court in 1945. In the hysteria of early 1945, with the Reich facing defeat, to be hauled in front of such a court usually meant death.

Chapter 2
Resistance

During the early years of the Nazi regime resistance was uncoordinated, allowing Hitler to consolidate his grip on German society. During World War II the only effective resistance came from the military, which bungled several assassination attempts.

*G*estapo archives reveal that between 1933 and 1945 some 800,000 people were incarcerated on charges of resistance within the Third Reich. Yet Hitler's grip on power was almost impregnable from his appointment as Chancellor in 1933, until the second he shot himself on 30 April 1945. Discussion about anti-Nazi resistance has to reckon with this fundamental truth. At no point was the Nazi regime seriously threatened by resistance action. What we have to reconcile is the large number of resisters with their limited political impact.

The traditional resistance movement within Nazi Germany was the political left – communists and socialists. Even before Operation Barbarossa, the invasion of Russia, in 1941, Nazis and communists were locked in conflict. From 1921 Germany saw literal street battles between Hitler's brown-shirted thugs of the *Sturmabteilung* (SA; Storm Detachment) and communist cells operating within Germany's major cities, as the two ideologies vied for influence over urban districts.

But the pre-1933 communist resistance to Nazism was primarily

Below: Otto Wels, leader of the SPD until its dissolution by the Nazis in 1933. He went into exile in Prague until 1938, and then later fled to Paris. He is seen here giving a speech in Berlin, 6 March 1932.

democratic. By 1932 the *Kommunistische Partei Deutschlands* (KPD; Communist Party of Germany) had a membership of 300,000. As Germany's main communist political party since 1918, the KPD solidly appealed to working-class interests and was a genuine contender for government. Its Achilles heel was its separation from other left-wing political parties, particularly with the *Socialdemokratische Partei Deutschlands* (SPD; Social Democratic Party of Germany). The SPD appealed to the same class interests as the KPD, although with a less radical edge to their politics. In the elections of November 1932, the Nazi Party brought in 33.1 percent of the vote, while the KPD had 16.9 percent and the SPD 20.4 percent. Between them the left-wing parties netted 221 seats in the *Reichstag* to the Nazis' 196, the NSDAP (the Nazi Party) actually losing 34 seats. Yet ideological enmities prevented a dominant left-wing coalition. The KPD classed the SPD as little more than a fascist organization, while the SPD mistrusted the KPD's Stalinism.

Left: A communist KPD poster for the 1932 elections. Its rather naive message is "Away with the system", a swipe at the von Papen regime. The KPD hated the SPD almost as much as it did the Nazis.

Although the KPD and SPD remained alienated, they were strong enough to concern Hitler. As he took the Chancellorship in 1933, he acted with characteristic brutality. *Gestapo* and SA units raided KPD headquarters, arresting leaders and acquiring the extensive and well-kept lists of party members and donators

Below: The trial of Marius van der Lubbe, who was accused of starting the *Reichstag* fire of February 1933. He was tried publicly and sentenced to death, despite the fact that he was half-blind and retarded.

Left: The scene in the *Bürgerbräukeller* following the explosion of the bomb planted by Georg Elser, 8 November 1939. Quickly apprehended, Elser was finally shot by the SS in April 1945.

so useful in the following witch-hunt. Entire districts of Berlin and other cities were purged of communist elements. Around 8000 communists escaped abroad. Those who fell into Nazi hands faced an awful future: execution, torture or incarceration in early concentration camps, such as the one at Dachau.

Matters worsened for the communists after a supposed act of anti-Nazi resistance. On 27 February 1933, the German *Reichstag* was damaged by an incendiary bombing. German police arrested a Dutchman, Marius van der Lubbe, a communist. It is now believed that the *Reichstag* fire was engineered by the SA, perhaps by Göring himself, to justify subsequent anti-communist policy. Hitler presented the fire as an attempted communist revolution, and persuaded President von Hindenburg to pass emergency legislation suspending key civil liberties and giving the police unprecedented powers of arrest and search. Some 30,000 left-wing activists were subsequently killed between 1933 and 1945.

Under this persecution how did the communists resist? A typical resistance organization was the Uhrig-Römer group. The group was named after the Berlin industrial worker Robert Uhrig and the KPD activist Josef "Beppo" Römer. Together they built up a resistance network producing anti-Nazi pamphlets and a bi-monthly magazine. They also engaged in minor industrial sabotage, particularly within arms production units. One factory alone contained some 80 activists. As many communist groups would find, however, spreading anti-Nazi literature left a traceable paper trail. Steadily the group was betrayed and revealed. Römer himself was arrested in February 1942, going to the guillotine in September 1944.

Resistance from the Uhrig-Römer group and others such as the Saefow-Jacob group, who applied similar methods, achieved minimal results. Under the Nazis' popular employment policies, traditional working-class loyalty towards communist ideals had dissolved, eroding the left-wing support base.

More crucially, the Molotov-Ribbentrop Pact of August 1939 bound the Soviet Union and Germany together in mutual military undertakings. Many communists were appalled at the association, while others welcomed the pact. It did not allow them respite from persecution, but their resistance activities did diminish. Michael Burleigh (in *The Third Reich – A New History*, Macmillan, 2000) points out that communists became so "inconsequential" that arrests went from 500 in January 1939 to only 70 in April 1940.

Nevertheless, not everyone gave in. One of the bolder acts of resistance came on 8 November 1939. The communist Georg Elser planted a bomb in the *Bürgerbräukeller* restaurant, Munich. Hitler was due to speak there, celebrating the *putsch* of 1923. Unfortunately for subsequent world history, Hitler arrived early, spoke for only a short time, then left. Thirteen minutes later the bomb went off,

killing eight Nazi supporters. Elser was apprehended and endured five years in concentration camps, but was finally executed by the *Gestapo* a short time before the war's end.

Left-wing resistance was not just a communist practice. Two other sectors of resistance lay in the SPD and German trade unions. The SPD was banned in 1933 and proved unable to coordinate its supporters in widespread resistance. Some SPD activists did pursue espionage, but they were in a minority and most members simply melted into Nazi society. However, a few individuals maintained an ideological resistance through discussion groups or occasional literature protests, brave acts in themselves when the slightest opposition to the Nazi Party could be a capital offence.

Trade union resistance was conducted along similar lines to that of the SPD. Trade unions were effectively dissolved as part of Hitler's political house-clearance when he took office, instead absorbing

Above: Soviet Foreign Minister Molotov (far left) in discussion with Hitler (right). The 1939 non-aggression pact between the two disillusioned German communists and weakened their anti-Nazi activities.

workers' representation into the Nazi-controlled *Deutsche Arbeitsfront* (DAF; German Labour Front). The vast majority of the 20 million workers working under the DAF did not pursue resistance projects. Yet substantial groups of unionists did form networks of anti-Nazi workers, particularly in transport and raw material industries. Although these networks did not destabilize the Nazi regime, had there been a political coup they would have been a very powerful force indeed.

The Red Orchestra

One other aspect to communist resistance was espionage. Not all communist resisters were confined to Germany's industrial base. Some occupied high positions in the German civil service, positions giving them access to privileged and sensitive information. The most famous clandestine group was the *Rote Kapelle* or "Red Orchestra". The Red Orchestra was a network of around 150 communist spies active within the German Government and military between 1938 and 1942, with cells throughout Europe. It included some notable personalities. There was Harro Schulze-Boysen, the grandson of Admiral Alfred von Tirpitz, and Avrid Harnack, nephew to the theologian Adolf von Harnack. A large part of the group's activity was the printing and distribution of leaflets exposing the appalling fate of the Jews. A sub-group in the Rhine-Ruhr area also started up a monthly protest newspaper (discovered and crushed by the *Gestapo* in 1943).

At its most effective the Red Orchestra engaged in high-level spying for the Soviet Union from within the German civil service. Following the German invasion of the Soviet Union in June 1941, the group faced constant demands from Moscow for up-to-date intelligence on German military manoeuvres. They managed to send a fairly constant flow of information about Germany's economic and social situation, and some privileged details

Above: Harro Schulze-Boysen (left), seen here as an employee of the Reich Ministry of Aviation, was a member of the communist Red Orchestra resistance group. He was hanged by the Nazis.

of future German military actions. Schulze-Boysen, for example, worked in the Reich Ministry of Aviation, with access to *Luftwaffe* operational plans. A major problem was establishing radio contact between Berlin and Moscow. Moscow assisted by parachuting agents into Germany, who helped to set up more efficient communication links. Now timely information was sent, and *Abwehr* estimates late in the war laid 200,000 German deaths at the door of Red Orchestra intelligence.

In August 1942, the Red Orchestra was broken by the *Abwehr*. Schulze-Boysen was arrested even as he attempted to send a message about all *Luftwaffe* deployments around Stalingrad. Typically for spies, their end was gruesome. Of 118 individuals sent to trial, 8 were hanged (often from meat hooks) and 41 were guillotined. The rest faced equally certain death within the concentration camps.

Youth resistance

The Nazi regime offered much to mobilize and inspire the impressionable German youth in the 1930s. Equally, the pressures placed upon youth culture to become super-fit, militaristic and violent-minded alienated many young people. A select few, therefore, became resisters, particularly those at university age, traditionally an age of rebelliousness.

Simply enjoying cultural practices at odds with Nazi cultural doctrine was one form of youth resistance. Dance and jazz music imported from Great Britain and the US, for example, inspired many youth groups, despite it falling under the category of "degenerate" art in Nazi thought. The swing youth and Edelweiss Pirates were two such groups, representing middle- and working-class communities respectively. The Edelweiss Pirates

Left: Arvid Harnack was a member of the Red Orchestra. He was sentenced to death for treason and was garroted at Plötzensee on Christmas Eve, 1942. His wife was beheaded on 16 February 1943.

were especially active. They would dress in colourful shorts, checked shirts and neck ties, and adopted local group names such as "Navajos". Their boisterous behaviour sometimes involved attacking Hitler Youth groups, often during the camping and hiking expeditions they organized to escape the Nazi surveillance in urban areas.

The members of such groups were frequently incarcerated, or worse, by the Nazis. On 7 December 1942 alone, for example, 28 groups in Düsseldorf containing 729 young people were broken up, and all ringleaders hanged. Persecution increased as the young people became more politicized. One infamous group of youngsters was the Helmuth Hubener group. Hubener was the 16-year-old leader of a small group of resisters. They printed their own leaflets attacking National Socialist doctrine, and also published and distributed illegal transcripts of British Broadcasting Corporation (BBC) transmissions. Despite their extreme youth, when caught the Hubener gang were shown no mercy. Hubener himself was beheaded, while the other

31

members of the group disappeared into prisons and concentration camps.

The White Rose group is probably the most famous of the youth activists. It was a group of university students at the University of Munich who practised passive resistance against the Third Reich. Their principal objective was to alert ordinary Germans to Nazi barbarity. Of this several members of White Rose had personal experience. Founding members Hans Scholl and Alexander Schmorell had served in the German Army in Poland and the Soviet Union, there witnessing the slaughter of entire Jewish communities by the *Einsatzgruppen*. Likewise, Willi Graf – another key member – had been a medical orderly in France and Yugoslavia in 1940–41, seeing the true meaning of Nazi occupation.

These three, along with others such as Hans' sisters Sophie and Inge, Christoph Probst, Jürgen Wittenstein and Kurt Huber, began a programme of leaflet distribution. Their methods were modelled closely on those used by the black civil rights community in the United States. Leaflets were targeted at individuals whom the group felt were suited to spreading the message further: university lecturers, teachers, doctors and even public house landlords. Names were selected out of telephone books, the leaflets published on a hand-cranked printing press, then stuffed laboriously into individual envelopes and posted. The effort required a huge volume of stamps, and the group had to be cautious about purchasing too many from a single shop in case it aroused suspicion.

The text of the leaflets was passionate but rational, and capably tapped into buried guilt about the Jews. Here is a passage from their second leaflet (they produced six leaflets in total):

Below: Piles of dead Jews at Belsen concentration camp. The White Rose tried to alert the German people to the horrors being committed by the Nazis in their name, especially in the Soviet Union.

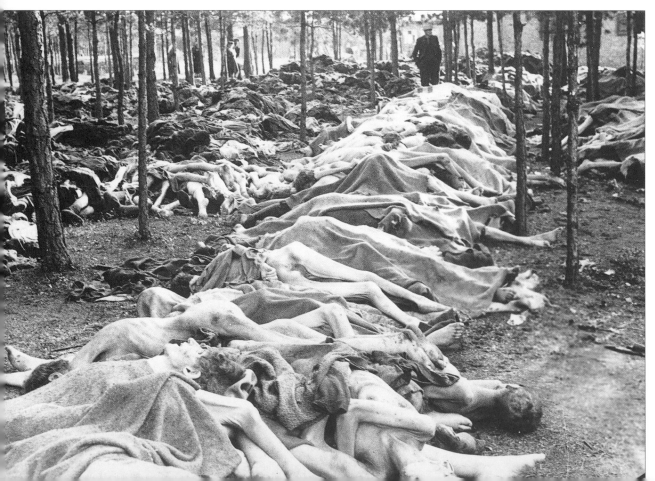

Left: The White Rose tried to unveil Nazi lies. For example, this is Terezin concentration camp, which was used during the war by the Nazis to make the International Red Cross believe that Terezin was a spa town.

We do not want to discuss here the question of the Jews, nor do we want in this leaflet to compose a defence or apology. No, only by way of example do we want to cite the fact that since the conquest of Poland 300,000 Jews have been murdered in this country in the most bestial way. Here we see the most frightful crime against human dignity, a crime that is unparalleled in the whole of history. For Jews, too, are human beings.

The *Gestapo* made the arrest of the White Rose a number-one priority as the group's activities became bolder. In February 1943 Hans, Alex and Willi painted huge anti-Nazi slogans on houses along Ludwigstrasse, a major Munich thoroughfare. Then, on 18 February, Hans and Sophie Scholl took a large suitcase full of leaflets (the sixth in their series) to the university. They distributed them

around empty lecture halls, soon to be filled with students, but also, impetuously, threw handfuls from a third-floor window into a courtyard. They were spotted by Jakob Schmidt, a Nazi supporter, who immediately contacted the *Gestapo*. Within minutes they were arrested.

On 20 February 1943, Hans and Sophie Scholl and Christoph Probst

Below: Roland Freisler, President of the People's Court, who tried the members of the White Rose group. Hitler's favourite legal executioner, he often unleashed a stream of vitriol against defendants.

were tried before the infamous and sadistic People's Court judge Roland Freisler. Within a few hours of the end of the trial – the outcome a foregone conclusion – all three had been beheaded. Inge Scholl and her parents were imprisoned. Alexander Schmorell, Willi Graf, Jürgen Wittenstein and Kurt Huber also met death in the coming weeks, and 80 other people associated with the White Rose group were incarcerated. Sophie's final words, recorded by Else Gebel who shared Sophie's cell, are a touching mix of idealistic strength and naiveté: "It is such a splendid sunny day, and I have to go. But how many have to die on the battlefield in these days, how many young, promising lives. What does my death matter if by our acts thousands are warned and alerted."

Of all the resistance groups within Nazi Germany, by far the most significant in practical terms were the conservative élite and the military officer class. These two groups were effectively one, and represented resistance at the very heart of German military and civil service institutions.

Hitler's Nazi regime offended Germany's traditional élites (here given the imperfect label "conservatives") on many different levels. Nazi authoritarianism was not the essential problem – many German Conservatives themselves approved of authoritarian dictatorships and had opposed the liberalism of the Weimar Republic. Yet much about Hitler's ideology and administration attacked core conservative values. Hitler loathed the trappings of Prussian aristocracy, and created his party around many individuals the conservatives deemed as thuggish or servile. Conservative civil servants and military officers suffered under Hitler's re-ordered administration. Hitler was fond of creating departments with

Below: Architects of the 1938 Munich Agreement (from left to right): Chamberlain, Daladier, Hitler, Mussolini and Ciano. Hitler's bloodless victory diffused active military resistance.

Left: Not all German university students were left-wing enemies of the Nazis. These Berlin University undergraduates show their active support for Hitler's regime.

Below: Franz von Papen (second from left) was a notable conservative who criticized the regime in 1934. Weak and ineffectual, he apologized for his remarks and was made ambassador to Austria.

overlapping responsibilities, in turn generating interdepartmental rivalries while consolidating Hitler's absolute authority. Many conservatives were not prepared to do the toadying required to get into Hitler's favour. Most importantly, conservative resistance snowballed or intensified as Germany lurched towards defeat between 1942 and 1945. The élite, quite simply, did not want to ally themselves with a regime heading for destruction.

Much conservative resistance was of a passive or ideological type. In 1934, for example, a group motivated

35

Left: Count von Moltke of the Kreisau Circle, an anti-Nazi conservative group. Von Moltke is seen here at his trial in January 1945, at which he received a death sentence, and was later hanged.

by the talented conservative lawyer Edgar Julius Jung started to mobilize support against the Nazis. One member of this group was Franz von Papen, a former German Chancellor who assisted Hitler's rise to power and became Hitler's Vice-Chancellor in 1933. Disillusioned by the Nazis' brutal methods (von Papen lost many close friends in the purge of the SA in June 1934), he delivered a famous speech crafted by Jung at the University of Marburg on 17 June 1934. The speech criticized Nazi one-party politics and its racial theories – von Papen was an advocate of integrating with Europe rather than conquering it. It was hoped that the speech might trigger a military coup, but this did not materialize (the *Gestapo* rigorously controlled the distribution of the speech). Instead, von Papen apologized for the speech and, showing remarkable survival skills, became Minister to Vienna, overseeing the *Anschluss*. Others were not so fortunate. Following further speeches delivered by group members, the *Gestapo* clamped down: Jung and many other key conservative thinkers such as Herbert von Bose and Erich Klausener were dead within weeks.

Another important group of conservative resisters was the Kreisau Circle, a small group of officers and professionals who formed an opposition movement in 1933 as Hitler ascended to power. The group was named after the estate of Helmut James Graf von Moltke, the legal advisor to the German military high command, at Kreisau in Silesia where many of the group's meetings where held. Although the group contained diverse philosophies, almost all were united in a Christian conservatism. They desired an end to Nazi atrocities and a new government, the rationale of which was laid out in a document entitled *Basic Principles for the New Order* drafted on 9 August 1942. Von Moltke summarized the essence of the group in a letter to his wife in October 1943: "In France extensive shootings are going on as I write. And all that is child's play compared to what is happening in Poland and Russia. How can I bear this and sit just the same in my warm room and drink teas?"

Despite these sentiments, in many senses the Kreisau Circle was little more than a debating chamber. The professional stature and influence, however, of some of its members meant that there were resisters at the heart of the Nazi establishment. These would in turn give leverage to the efforts of the most important group of resisters, military officers.

Military resistance

The durability of Hitler and his regime is all the more remarkable when considering the list of military luminaries on the side of the resistance. A quick roll call includes

Ludwig Beck (Chief of Staff of the German Armed Forces, 1935–38), Admiral Wilhelm Canaris (director of the *Abwehr*, the counterintelligence branch of the German high command, 1935–44), General Franz Halder (Chief of the General Staff of the German Army, 1938–42), and Field Marshal Erwin Rommel (one of Germany's most successful wartime commanders). Even head of the SS Heinrich Himmler, after Hitler the man most closely identified with the Nazi regime, participated in activities which fall into the category of resistance. Why was the resistance so prevalent amongst such powerful men?

Reasons are not hard to find. From 1934 onwards Hitler increasingly centralized military command within his own control, sucking strategic authority away from the generals. On 4 February 1938 he created the *Oberkommando der Wehrmacht*, a new layer of military authority with strategic jurisdiction over the various German arms of service. Hitler was already (from 1934) the supreme commander of the German forces; creating the OKW merely formalized

his strategic pre-eminence. From 1938, generals and field marshal were all too often relegated to secondary tacticians, and the officer class was infuriated at what it saw as an ill-informed World War I corporal making decisions about the deployment of the forces.

During the early days of the Nazi campaign in World War II – when

Germany was militarily ascendant (in no small part, it has to be said, to Hitler's strategic talent) – this relationship worked reasonably. However, following the invasion of the Soviet Union in June 1941, Hitler and his generals were increasingly at loggerheads. Relations plummeted after the German disaster at Kursk in July 1943. Hitler, his spirits low after the defeat of the Sixth Army at Stalingrad, turned strategic decisions regarding Kursk over to the capable Field Marshal Erich von Manstein. Kursk turned into a German catastrophe, and Hitler felt confirmed in regarding the officer class as politically unreliable, strategically cautious and obtrusive. He became over imperious in his strategic control, and resistance thickened. Interestingly, von Manstein had actually belonged in the resistance camp. During 1942 he held discussions with resistance leaders Colonel-General Ludwig Beck and Major-General Henning von Tresckow, and agreed to the principle of assassinating Hitler. Von Manstein renounced this view after the German defeat at Stalingrad, and remained loyal to the Führer for the rest of the war.

Military opposition

So how did the German military establishment oppose the Nazi regime? On one level, we see German Army leaders being tardy or downright stubborn over implementing Hitler's orders. The redoubtable General Guderian, for example, almost openly defied Hitler's redeployment orders during the winter campaign in the Soviet Union in 1941. (It should be noted that Guderian was never a member of the resistance movement, just an officer striving for campaign success.) Military historians such as the late Alan Clark have seen in such acts of disobedience the real roots of

German failure on the Eastern Front. Such a view is debatable, but certainly Hitler's orders were subject to interpretation or delay. At the opposite extreme is the cases of German units, even SS units, in 1945 refusing outright to obey Hitler's final, suicidal attack orders. These cases, however, are almost entirely confined to the very last weeks of the war when defeat was certain.

Some military leaders also "resisted" Hitler's regime by either betraying secrets to the enemy or negotiating with the Allies without Hitler's permission or knowledge. Such resistance went very high indeed up the Nazi chain of command. Admiral Canaris, the head

Above: Field Marshal Erich von Manstein, one of the most able German commanders of World War II. Initially willing to listen to anti-Hitler officers in the army, he ultimately stayed loyal to the regime.

of the *Abwehr*, fed information to the Allies about Hitler's war plans between 1939 and 1941, attempted to stop certain acts of genocide against Jews and Russians, and later participated in the planned assassination of Hitler by the staff of Army Group Centre in March 1943. Heinrich Himmler, effectively the second most powerful man in the Nazi regime, did not betray intelligence, but during 1945 secretly attempted to negotiate peace with the Allies behind Hitler's back. The illicit activities of both Canaris and Himmler were ultimately unveiled. Canaris was executed in April 1945, having been implicated in the July 1944 bomb plot. Himmler was dismissed from his posts but his previously impeccable Nazi credentials saved him from execution (he died by his own hand after capture by the Allies).

Assassination attempts

Assassination plots and attempts against Hitler accompanied his reign from the beginning. Despite numerous actual attempts, a mixture of Hitler's remarkable good fortune and the planning inefficiencies of the conspirators meant Hitler survived them all.

The first serious assassination plot by a high-ranking group of officers was in 1938. A group of conspirators led by General Franz Halder (Chief of the Army General Staff), and including the *Abwehr* chief of staff Major General Hans Oster and former president of the *Reichsbank* Dr Hjalmar Schacht, planned a military coup in Berlin. Halder and many others were horrified at Hitler's decision to plunge Germany into war, and Halder took a gun along to his meetings with Hitler, waiting for the right moment to strike. Unfortunately, Germany's agreement with Neville Chamberlain, the British prime minister, at Munich signed on

30 September 1938 stole much of the rationale for the plot, and the idea, if not the intent, was put on hold.

The Halder plot was just the beginning of military assassination plans. In July 1940, for example, *Oberleutnant* d. R. Fritz-Dietlof Graf von der Schulenburg and Dr Eugen Gerstenmaier planned to kill Hitler during the Paris victory parade, but the plot never came to fruition. A far more realistic attempt came in March 1943 when Hitler returned home from Smolensk after a trip to review the Eastern Front campaign. A group of three Army Group Centre conspirators – Major-General Henning von Tresckow, *Leutnant* Fabian von Schlabrendorff and *Oberst* Rudolf-Christoph Freiherr von Gersdorff – placed a bomb disguised

Above: Russian tanks at the Battle of Kursk, July 1943. This German defeat further confirmed Hitler's view that the German officer corps was unreliable and inept.

as a bottle of brandy on Hitler's aircraft, a Focke-Wulf 200 Condor. Success seemed assured as Hitler's aircraft took off for the home flight to Germany, the timer due to detonate the bomb during that flight. A devilish hand seemed to protect Hitler once again; the timer initiated the detonation sequence but failed to trigger the explosives. March 1943 saw numerous other attempts on Hitler's life, all foiled by bad luck or failures in planning.

The 1944 bomb plot

Hitler was not so lucky in July 1944. By this time the anti-Hitler faction within high-ranking military circles was very powerful indeed. From their midst emerged one Colonel Claus Schenk Graf von Stauffenberg. Following a combat injury in Tunisia in April 1943, von Stauffenberg became chief of staff of the General Army Office in October 1943, in June 1944 also becoming the chief of staff to the commanding officer (Freidrich Fromm) of the Reserve Army. By 1944, von Stauffenberg was already complicit with conspirators such as von Tresckow and Beck. He had met these men while attending meetings at Hitler's forest headquarters, known as the "Wolf's Lair", near Rastenburg in East Prussia. It was here that von Stauffenberg implemented Operation Valkyrie.

Valkyrie was planned in early 1944, as the situation on the Eastern Front spiralled into disaster for the Germans. Von Stauffenberg intended to place a suitcase bomb next to Hitler during a conference scheduled for 20 July. Von Stauffenberg would make his excuses and leave, the bomb would kill Hitler, and the conspirators would simultaneously use their military influence to take control of the German government and infrastructure in Berlin.

On 20 July 1944, amidst tight security, von Stauffenberg made his way into the meeting room, a large wooden hut serving as a conference chamber. There he met the Führer, shook hands, and surreptitiously placed the suitcase containing 1kg (2.2lb) of plastic explosive on the floor beside Hitler. Von Stauffenberg then left the room, claiming the need to make a phone call. While he was out, one of the room's 24 occupants, Colonel Heinz Brandt, moved the suitcase further under the table to make more space, pushing it against the concrete roof support which would save Hitler's life.

The bomb detonated at 12:50 hours, completely shattering the

Above: Henning von Tresckow, the senior operations officer of Army Group Centre who played a major part in the 1944 bomb plot. On hearing of its failure, he committed suicide.

building. Inside the hut, one man was killed instantly and numerous others severely wounded – three men, including Brandt, would later die from their wounds. Hitler had burns to the right leg and his head, his right arm was partially paralyzed, and he suffered damaged hearing. He was alive, however. Of this fact von Stauffenberg was unaware as he flew back to the War Ministry in Berlin to arrange the subsequent takeover. He believed that all the occupants of the hut had been killed, such was the devastation. Yet it was the flimsy construction of the hut which allowed the explosion to dissipate its force rather than be contained within its walls. (Unfortunately, the original venue of the meeting – an underground concrete bunker – was being redecorated, hence the relocation to the wooden hut.) Only on von Stauffenberg's arrival in Berlin did he learn the truth.

Hitler exacted a terrible revenge. Some 200 conspirators were hunted down and murdered. Von Stauffenberg and four others were shot at midnight the same day. Ludwig Beck attempted suicide, but bungled it and was shot by an army sergeant. Others were later strangled by piano wire while hanging from meat hooks. Hitler even had these deaths filmed, and watched them at his leisure.

Hitler's widespread revenge swept away many of the key military conspirators arraigned against him, including Canaris, Rommel and von Tresckow. The most serious attempt on Hitler's life had, by evil irony, probably consolidated his power even as Germany collapsed into total destruction.

Resistance from the Christian community in Germany was fairly minor. Hitler and the Nazis had little but contempt for religion. They refrained from outright religious persecution as Christian beliefs were still widespread in German society, and Hitler found it more useful to channel these beliefs into a kind of religious and militaristic nationalism rather than crush them. In 1933 Hitler agreed a concordat with the papacy that in return for Hitler granting Catholics freedom of worship, Rome would not intrude into the political life of the Third Reich. Having agreed this, German Christianity was then absorbed under the "German Faith" organization headed by the "Reich Bishop" Ludwig Müller. German Faith did not endear itself to other Christians, especially after it banned the Old Testament because of its Jewish content.

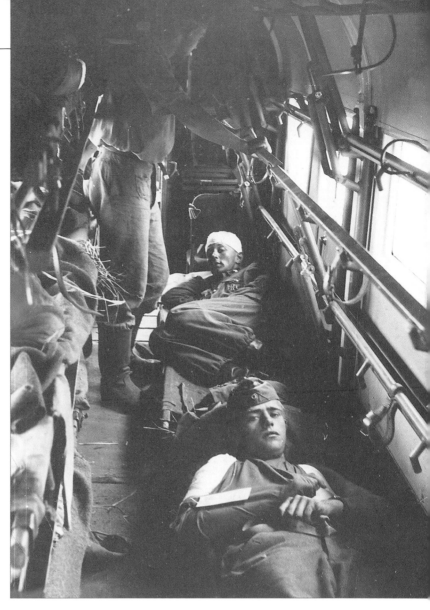

Above: Wounded German soldiers being evacuated from Stalingrad. One thing that galvanized military resistance against Hitler was the appalling losses being suffered on the Eastern Front.

Above: German
troops parade
through occupied
Paris. Such military
victories firmly
cemented support
for Hitler among the
vast majority of the
German people and
military up until the
end of the war.

Left: A Focke-Wulf
200, the type Hitler
used to fly to and
from the Eastern
Front. Hitler viewed
the officer corps as
incompetent, a view
reinforced by their
bungled attempts to
blow up his aircraft.

Objection to Jewish persecution
was the biggest single cause of
religious resistance to the Nazis.
Even before the German Faith
bisection of the Bible, thousands of
Protestant Christians had joined the
Emergency League, a religious group
headed by Martin Niemöller opposed
to National Socialist racial doctrine.
This group grew even larger after the
banning of the Old Testament (Saint
Paul was also excluded from the
German Faith Bible).

In 1934 the Emergency League
became known as the
Bekenntniskirche, or Confessional
Church. The Confessional Church
had a membership of 7000 Protestant
pastors, and organized its first
National Synod in May 1934. The
famous theologian Dietrich
Bonhöffer was one of its members.
Bonhöffer not only resisted on a
religious level through lectures and
writings, and by rescuing Jews, but he
also liaised with conspirators such as
Beck and Canaris for the overthrow
of Hitler. His associations eventually
caught up with him. He was arrested
by the *Gestapo* after the July 1944 plot

and was eventually executed in Flossenbürg concentration camp on 9 April 1945.

Bonhöffer's fate was to befall many in the Confessional Church, and they were rarely more than a minor irritation to the Nazis. Some did manage to have an impact on Nazi policy, though. The Bishop of Münster, Clemens Graf von Galen, for example, protested in 1941 about the Nazi extermination of the mentally disabled and caused Hitler to stop the killings, or at least mask them from the German public.

But von Galen was an exception. The Nazis had no compunction about persecuting rebellious Christians, and many Christians understandably chose to keep themselves and their families in safety rather than risk a one-way journey to Buchenwald or Dachau. Many Christian groups actively supported Hitler's political, military and even racial campaigns. Following the German success in Poland, German bishops held a victory celebration even though Polish

Catholic clergy had been executed in Nazi atrocities. In 1935 the Fulda Bishops' Conference reassured the government that it "rejects all subversive attitudes and conduct, refrains from any political activity and especially will absolutely repel all attempted approaches of communism" (Burleigh, p.233). With such voices, German Christianity had little to contribute to large-scale resistance against the Nazi regime.

It is all too easy, however, to be disparaging about the state of German resistance between the early 1930s and 1945 when speaking from a position of safety. The German people were subject to the persuasions of a regime with first-rate propaganda tools and strategies at its disposal, backed up by the most awful instruments of state policing. There are doubtless many individual acts of resistance left untold, but equally we must accept that Hitler to a large extent dragged Germany to destruction with the general compliance of the German people.

Above: Pope Pius XII, who as an adviser to Pope Pius XI was instrumental in negotiating the concordat with the Nazis in 1933. He became pope in 1939 but stayed silent on Nazi atrocities.

Chapter 3
Culture and propaganda

Under the Nazis the arts were subverted to serve the interests of state ideology. The spectacular achievements of Weimar Culture were undone as artists were either forced to flee Germany or produce works that had the Nazi seal of approval.

Between the end of World War I (1914–18) and the assumption of power by the Nazis, German art and culture experienced a phenomenal renaissance. The causes were twofold. First, there was the collapse of the "old order". Prior to 1918, the Prussian monarchy had attempted to restrain artistic development, albeit not always successfully, through royal patronage of conservative and establishment tastes. However, once

the Kaiser went into exile in Holland in November 1918, the handbrake of "court culture" was removed and it became easier for artists to move in new directions. That many chose to take advantage of this opportunity was the result of the second factor, World War I. The overpowering experience of the Great War, with its extreme sights, sounds and emotions, inspired artists to new heights of creativity. The sensory overload they

Left: An example of the work of Walter Gropius. He exerted a major influence on the development of modern architecture and founded the Bauhaus, the German school of design, architecture and applied arts.

experienced through four years of conflict was channelled into works of art that exhibited a new dynamism and a willingness to experiment with radically modern themes and forms of expression.

Consequently, Weimar Culture (the artistic output of the years 1919 to 1933) was of an exceptional standard, and outstanding new work appeared in all fields. Innovative music was composed by the likes of Arnold Schönberg, Kurt Weill and Hanns Eisler. Great theatrical works were written by playwrights such as

Bertold Brecht; and exciting novels by authors including Erich Kästner, Erich Maria Remarque and the brothers Thomas (who was awarded the Nobel Prize for Literature in 1929) and Heinrich Mann. There were ground-breaking historical studies by scholars such as Eckart Kehr, while emotive sculptures and drawings were produced by artists including Käthe Kollwitz, who became the first woman to be elected a member of the Prussian Academy of Arts. Beautiful furniture and household objects were designed by

Above: The Nazi exhibition of "degenerate art" that opened in Munich on 4 March 1936. It went on tour in Germany from the summer of 1937. The exhibition enjoyed great success – it was one of the few opportunities Germans had to appreciate good art.

Walter Gropius, Marcel Breuer and the Bauhaus at the same time as breathtaking buildings by architects such as Mies van der Rohe were erected (his monument to the Spartacists Karl Liebknecht and Rosa Luxemburg in Berlin, erected in 1926, would not have endeared him to the Nazis). Fritz Lang made original films, such as *Destiny* (1920), and, all in all, it was an almost unprecedented outpouring of talent that looked set to turn Germany into the artistic and cultural dynamo of Europe.

With the coming to power of the Nazis in January 1933, the creative flow was halted. Hitler had nothing but contempt for Weimar Culture,

which the Führer likened to a "junkyard", and immediate plans were made to sweep much of it away. In part, the consequent purge was a reflection of National Socialist taste. Very few of the top Nazi leaders had any real understanding of art and culture. Hitler, for example, had twice been refused entry to art school in Vienna before World War I. The Nazis were particularly at a loss when it came to appreciating modernism or the avant-garde. Striking out at what they did not understand, they labelled as "subversive" anything that did not adhere slavishly to the most traditional styles. Thus, expressionist painting, cubism and atonal forms of

Left: Minister for Public Enlightenment and Propaganda Josef Goebbels (second from left) visits the exhibition of "degenerate art" in Berlin on 27 February 1938.

Left: Hitler at a concert in the late 1930s. Music in Nazi Germany had to conform to the traditionalist tastes of Hitler and the Nazi élite. These included the works of Richard Wagner and Carl Orff.

music were removed from art galleries and museums or banned from being performed in theatres and concert halls. The only exception was when such works were wheeled out for exhibitions of "degenerate culture". These were designed to show how the Nazis had saved Germany from the "disease" and "cultural anarchy" that was Weimar art. In 1938, for example, an exhibition was held of "degenerate" music. On display were exhibits highlighting the supposed "barbarian" qualities of jazz and the "complete spiritual cretinization" of avant-garde orchestral composition.

"Degenerate" art

Similarly, in 1937, some 700 modernist masterpieces were gathered together in an exhibition in the *Antikenmuseum* in Munich, the intent of which was made abundantly clear by a catalogue that printed photographs of the modernist works beside the drawings of schizophrenia patients. Evidently, the public was supposed to recognize the "similarities" between the two, equate modernism with a "disturbed" mind and appreciate their debt to the regime for saving them from spiritual degradation. Whether the German public actually did so is open to question. Some two million people attended the Munich exhibition, which suggested that many were visiting to appreciate the art rather than to denigrate it. Tellingly, the regime's next big "degenerate" art exhibition was the public destruction of some 5000 "un-German" paintings and drawings in front of Berlin's main fire station.

In spite of such acts of wanton vandalism, it would be wrong to assume that the Nazi purge of German intellectual and artistic life was purely the product of the deep-rooted cultural philistinism of the party leaders. While many Nazi

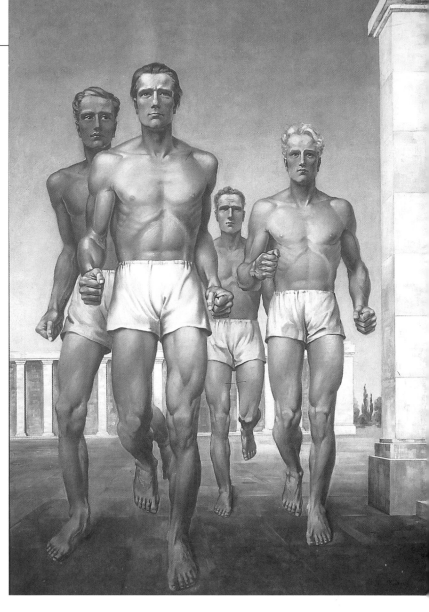

bigwigs may have been thick-skulled thugs who leapt at the chance to destroy works of art they did not understand, the National Socialist authorities had more sinister purposes in mind. As part of their broader plan to mould Germany in their image, the Nazis intended to use German cultural life as a means of transmitting their message. To do this, German art needed to be stripped of those elements that contradicted National Socialist ideology. Accordingly, the Nazis selected the artists and artistic works to be purged not only on the basis of their simplistic tastes, but also against two very specific, albeit artistically irrelevant, criteria.

Above: The type of artistic image the Nazis approved of – perfect examples of German Aryan men undertaking sports. This picture, entitled "Gymnasts", was painted by Gerhard Keil in 1939.

The first was the concept of the *Volk*, that is to say race and nation. The Nazis viewed the world through the bigoted eyes of a racist ideology that placed primacy on the achievements of the Nordic "Aryan" people. Given this outlook it is hardly surprising that, on coming to power, they decided that one of their first acts would be to "liberate" German culture from foreign – and especially Jewish – influence. Works that were not deemed racially sound were consigned to the flames. Huge bonfires, fuelled by the books and manuscripts of Jewish and other "un-German" artists, were constructed in all the major cities. With the blacklist of "undesirable" books running to more than 10,000 titles, this process denuded whole libraries of their classic German literature. The poems of Heinrich Heine, who after Goethe and Schiller was probably the greatest German poet of all time, were burned on the grounds that the author was Jewish. Musical scores of the extraordinary German-Jewish composer Felix Mendelssohn were taken from the nation's conservatories and orchestras and consigned to the flames because of his racial background. Observing such events, many artists of Jewish ancestry fled the country for friendlier shores. Those who stayed found that they could no longer find an audience for their work. They would soon be unable to work at all.

The second criterion against which artists were measured was their political allegiance. Many of the most prominent cultural figures of the Weimar period were supporters of left-wing political parties, and as such were considered by the Nazis to be ideological enemies. Accordingly, their works were branded

Above: Nazi architecture rejected modern style. Official Nazi policy required a monumental neo-classical design for big buildings. This is the outside of the giant Olympic Stadium in Berlin.

Kulturbolschewismus (cultural Bolshevism) and attacked as decadent, degenerate and, inevitably, "un-German". This had severe consequences for the artists, who were subject to acts of ill-treatment and persecution. Many took the prudent step of leaving the country, producing an exodus of talent including Bertold Brecht, Kurt Weill and the brothers Mann. Those who remained in Germany often found themselves and their work under constant critical, if not actual, assault from the new regime. Expelled from prestigious cultural organizations and denied a venue for their work, many abandoned their art for the duration of Nazi rule.

Ridding German intellectual and cultural life of such so-called "pernicious and undesirable" elements was not the full extent of the Nazi programme. There was also the small matter of filling with new material the artistic void that had been created by the purges. This was a process over which the Nazis maintained the tightest possible control. Accordingly, art and culture were subjected to the same overseeing technique that was used in all other walks of life – *Gleichschaltung*: that is, "coordination" or "incorporation". This meant state supervision of the arts, with dedicated organs being set up to coordinate German culture along proper National Socialist lines and incorporate it ideologically within the Nazi machine.

The Reich Chamber of Culture

Foremost among these new organizations was the *Reichskulturkammer* (Reich Chamber of Culture). This body, which was directly responsible to the Ministry of Propaganda, was sub-divided into seven departments, each of which oversaw a sphere of German cultural life. There was one department for literature, another for the news media, and one each for radio, the theatre, music, the visual arts and cinema. These sub-divisions exercised effective control over the entire corpus of German culture, by issuing clear instructions regarding those styles that were permitted and informing artists as to the type of work they were expected to produce. Political considerations were of paramount importance in deciding this, with the Nazis making it clear from the outset that the themes and ideas that artists explored in their cultural products had to be ones that promoted the party's core political beliefs.

Above: The inside of the Olympic Stadium in Berlin. Despite their rejection of the modern style, the Nazis often used the most advanced building techniques hidden behind neoclassical facades.

49

As the Nazis believed in the superiority of Aryan people over all others, this message was one that artists had to incorporate into their works. The manner in which this was achieved is illustrated by the types of sculpture that appeared in the Nazi period. Basically, all carved or moulded three-dimensional representations of the human form – that is to say, of German people – depicted an idealized race of physically perfect supermen. Being cast in the Hellenistic style of ancient Greece, these images depicted Germans not just as modern-day heroes but also as the heirs to Europe's greatest cultural and imperial tradition, that of Alexander the Great and of Caesar.

The Nazis also believed that struggle was good for the nation and that war, as the toughest of all tests, was a major engine of national

progress. Culture was therefore expected to reflect this concept. Nowhere was this more apparent than in literature. Books on the Great War, for example, were not permitted to focus on suffering, death and destruction. Instead, they had to be robustly masculine statements about the community of the trenches and the nobility, valour and heroism of the German soldier. Rather than decrying war for its evils, they were to promote it as a force for good.

The Nazis believed that a harmonious social paradise could be created in Germany with the formation of a *Volksgemeinschaft* based on *Blut und Boden* (blood and soil), which denoted a quasi-mystical connection between "blood" (the race or *Volk*) and "soil" (the land and the natural environment) specific to Germanic peoples, and notably absent among Jews, Celts and Slavs.

This notion of a domestic idyll also had to be incorporated into German art. It was in paintings that this was most often achieved. During the Nazi period, numerous studies appeared showing blissful rural scenes of families toiling together on the land, the men cultivating the fields and the women looking after hearth and home. With their emphasis on the sanctity of the soil and the blessings of female domesticity, these paintings promoted the Nazi message of a community linked by its ties of blood and united in its attachment to the Fatherland.

Given that the Nazis believed in the intrinsic grandeur of the German nation and the role of the party in cultivating this, art was expected to illustrate the power and self-confidence of the German people, and to demonstrate in tangible form how the Nazis had helped to achieve

Below: "Hitler at the Front" by Emil Scheibe. This painting is typical of the "heroic" style of Nazi art, which stressed the nobility of the German soldier. The harsh reality of war was a long way away.

this. As no cultural product is more instantly tangible than bricks and mortar, it was to architecture that the Nazis turned to give expression to this claim. The emphasis here was on gigantic, monumental buildings. Probably the most famous of these is the complex built at Nuremberg for the Nazi Party rallies. Nothing illustrates better the sense of how architecture could promote the message of German splendour than Nazi plans to transform Berlin into the new imperial capital city, "Germania". The plans set out deliberately to rival the glory of ancient Rome by building everything in the neo-classical style and on an enormous scale. Accordingly, the centrepiece of the scheme was to be a great hall, 16 times bigger than St Peter's in Rome, with a dome that rose 290m (951ft) into the air. It was to be an unmistakable, marble-clad statement of both the glory of the German people and the strength and permanence of the Nazi regime.

The death of creativity

The result of turning culture into a vehicle for ideological propaganda was to render much of it sterile and unimaginative. With art and learning required to fit a particular pattern, there was no need for originality. Creativity was quickly crowded out. This was as true for literature as it was for sculpture, and for architecture as it was for painting. Despite the atrophy that the Nazis caused in most fields, there was one area in which they were a more progressive force – cultural dissemination through modern audio-visual broadcast media. Radio, television and cinema gave them technologically sophisticated ways of spreading their message. They seized on these with alacrity, expanding the boundaries of modern broadcasting in the process.

Radio represents the classic example of the Nazis' enthusiastic promotion of modern mass media. With the *Reichsrundfunk Gesellschaft* (Reich Broadcasting Company) under strict state control, radio programmes represented an especially promising means of propagating the Nazi message. However, the success of this medium depended entirely on people's easy access to it. Accordingly, the Nazis made determined efforts to ensure that everyday exposure to the radio was achieved. Loudspeakers were installed in factories and other public places, making communal listening a popular activity. At the same time, eager to put what Minister for Propaganda Josef Goebbels called this "most modern instrument for influencing the masses" into every home, the regime prioritized production of cheap radio sets. The result was the "People's receiver 301". At RM35 it was cheap enough to ensure that radio ownership rose from 4 to 16 million people in less than a decade. This ensured mass exposure to the Nazi message, which was broadcast ceaselessly over the air waves. At the same time, Goebbels named the device so that it was a constant reminder of the date 30 January 1933, the day of the Nazi seizure of power. Even when switched off, it therefore served the interests of the regime.

Nazi television

As with radio, the Nazis were pioneers in the field of television. In 1935, they established the world's first regular broadcast service, a year ahead of both Great Britain and the US. Again, the motive was propaganda. Goebbels was looking for new ways of spreading Nazi ideology and saw the possibilities of television. As the medium was new and untested, the *Deutscher Fernseh-Rundfunk* (German Television Service) enjoyed the rare experience of being permitted to be innovative. Broadcasting mainly to special

Opposite: A Nazi night rally in Nuremberg. Night-time rallies, with torch-light parades, were designed to project Nazi power and create a magical atmosphere which would engulf the participants.

53

television parlours in Berlin, the programmers initially experimented with a diet of light entertainment comprising music, cookery, gardening and other domestic tabloid shows. With the development of better facilities and technical know-how, the schedule expanded to include live sport such as the Berlin Olympics and the European boxing championships, alongside specially commissioned dramas and news programming. In contrast with the British Broadcasting Corporation (BBC), which ceased its high-definition television service on the onset of war, the German service continued until 1944, breaking new technological and artistic boundaries in the process.

The Nazi regime was a great proponent of cinema for the usual propagandistic reasons. Goebbels

clearly recognized the ability of motion pictures "to mobilize emotions and immobilize minds", and developed German cinema accordingly. A huge investment in production took place during the Nazi period, ensuring that 1094 full-

Above: Cinema (top) and radio were mediums by which the Nazis could promote National Socialist ideology to ordinary Germans.

length feature films were made in Germany. There was also massive investment in infrastructure, with the number of cinemas rising from 5071 in 1933 to 7042 in 1942. During the same period, cinema admissions rose from 245 million individual visits in 1933 to more than a billion in 1942.

Nazi feature films

As these statistics show, the Germans were inveterate movie-goers. In one respect, this should have made films an ideal instrument for propaganda. For most Germans a trip to the cinema was a form of escapism. What people wanted was to be entertained, not to be bombarded with explicit political propaganda. Too much propaganda and people would probably stop going. With this in mind, the Nazis carefully choreographed the cinema experience. Part of the time was spent watching newsreels, in which information and propaganda were intimately intermixed. The rest of the time was spent watching a feature, in which any propaganda was made more subliminal. Of the 1094 films produced in Nazi Germany, 941 were comedies, musicals, dramas, detective films or adventure epics. Their purpose was to act as a distraction. Films were there to instil in Germans a sense of the normality of their surroundings and to suggest that life went on much as before. The less true this was – such as during the war years – the more important it became that films perpetuated this illusion.

While the majority of Nazi films were ordinary examples of popular entertainment, there were some productions of this era that rose above the mundane. Some stand out

Below: Aerial view of the 1936 Olympic Games in Berlin, the subject of Leni Riefenstahl's cinematic triumph *Olympia*. It was made with the full cooperation of the Nazi authorities.

as classics of the cinematic art. There are others that represent the worst monstrosities ever imprinted on celluloid. In the former category, best known are the works of the talented and controversial director Leni Riefenstahl, who created two electrifying depictions of Nazi mass rallies, *Triumph des Willens* (*Triumph of the Will*), a documentary study of the 1934 Nazi Party convention at Nuremberg that emphasized party unity, introduced the leaders to the German people, and exhibited Nazi power to the world and *Olympia*, a two-part film on the Olympic Games of 1936. Masterpieces of technical excellence in their use of camera work, understanding of light and shadow, and hypnotic portrayal of spectacle, they are of enduring fascination to film-makers today. At the other end of the spectrum are hate-inspired and poisonous films such as *Der ewige Jude* (*The Eternal Jew*), *Die Rothschilds* and, of course, *Jud Süss* (*Jew Süss*). The latter is without parallel in the history of

cinema. Such was the venom with which it depicted its central character, Jewish money-lender Joseph Süss Oppenheimer (and, by extension, all Jews), that it was shown to SS units to motivate them before they carried out murder operations against the Jews of Eastern Europe. As such, it can be considered an accessory to the

Above: A film theatre showing *Die Tänzerin von Sanssouci aka Barberina* with Lil Dagover, the "Grand Dame" of German film. Her films were light-hearted entertainment, rather than racist.

Left: The actor and director Veit Harlan in his starring role in *Jud Süss*. For his role in the film he was imprisoned by the Allies. In April 1949, he was found not guilty of "crimes against humanity" and released.

Above: Kristina Söderbaum (left), one of the Nazi regime's great female stars. Blonde and blue-eyed, she was married to Veit Harlan. Seen here in *Jud Süss*, she was acquitted by the Allies of war crimes.

Holocaust. This explains why its director, Veit Harlan, was indicted for Crimes against Humanity in the trials that followed the German surrender in 1945 (though exonerated by the court, he was black-listed after the war and had great difficulty finding employment for several years).

This notion of art as crime is the perfect epitaph for Nazi culture. At every level the National Socialist leadership turned what is supposed to be man's highest achievement into something sullied and base. This began with lies about their intentions for culture. Goebbels maintained in 1933 that the Nazis did "not wish to restrict, but rather to promote, art-cultural development". The Nazis then proceeded to demonstrate their cultural values by burning books, persecuting artists and quashing originality and creativity. Having done this, they turned their energies to making culture serve the autocratic state. Art was allowed to exist in National Socialist Germany only so long as it propagated the regime's message and instilled its values into ordinary people. Given the values of the National Socialist regime, this was a high price to pay for a precarious existence. Fascist art, as Susan Sontag explained, "glorifies surrender, it exalts mindlessness, it glamorizes death". With that as its role, it is small wonder that so many of the cultural products that emerged from Nazi Germany displayed such stultifying mediocrity. Neither is it surprising that it should have produced works, such as the film *Jud Süss*, that acted as an incitement to murder. As Ernest Bloch noted, the culture of the Third Reich acted like King Midas in reverse: everything it touched turned to dirt. The Nazis presided over the creation of a great deal of dirt, degradation and despair. That was the sum of their culture.

Chapter 4
Young Germans and Nazi youth policies

By thoroughly indoctrinating the young, the Nazis ensured a steady stream of loyal and reliable National Socialists. In the classroom the young were taught Nazi ideology, while outside school the Hitler Youth harnessed the young's enthusiasm.

For Hitler and the Nazis, influencing young people was a top priority. This reflected in part their preoccupation with the rejuvenation of the German race. The Nazis saw themselves as the builders of a "New Germany", and intended to forge a breed of Germans envisaged as a "master race". The raw material for this project, those who would be moulded into the "Aryan demi-gods" to rejuvenate the nation, would be the newest, most dynamic and malleable segment of the German population. Germany's children and adolescents were therefore of particular interest to the National Socialist leadership.

Compounding this ideological agenda, there were other motives behind the obsession with youth. Foremost was the need to bolster

Below: Adolf Hitler with members of the Hitler Youth in 1935. These youths are members of the German Young People organization, which was for boys between the ages of 10 and 14. Note the paramilitary attire.

Above: German youths throwing javelins. The Nazis promoted sports as a way of making their youth "as hard as Krupp steel".

Left: Hundreds of Hitler Youth members give Adolf Hitler a rapturous welcome upon his arrival at the 1935 Nuremberg rally.

support for the Nazis among the German people, as less than half had actually voted for the National Socialists in the March 1933 election. The Nazis were well aware that, over the long term, ensnaring the new generation was the key to ensuring majority support. If people could be turned into ardent National Socialists as children then it was almost certain that they would remain so as adults. This was Hitler's strategy. As he observed in a speech delivered on 6 November 1933: "When an opponent says, 'I will not come over to your side', I calmly say, your child belongs to us already … you will pass

59

on. Your descendants, however, now stand in the new camp. In a short time they will know nothing but this new community."

In addition to this domestic political calculation, young people were also an essential element in Hitler's foreign policy agenda, particularly his cherished goal of overrunning Europe in order to create *Lebensraum* (living space) for the German people (the Nazis believed that Germany was over-populated and needed more farmland to support itself, which would be taken from the "inferior" Slav peoples in the East). As this plan would entail territorial conquest on a vast scale, it required extensive military manpower. On the basis that the children of today are the soldiers of tomorrow, Hitler viewed Germany's youth with the needs of future war in mind. It was his intention that Germany's younger generation, without even knowing it, should be physically and mentally

prepared for conflict. He was speaking quite literally when he told the 1935 Nuremberg party rally that "what we look for from our German youth is different from what people wanted in the past. In our eyes the German youth of the future must be slim and slender, swift as the greyhound, tough as leather, and hard as Krupp steel." In short, they were expected to develop all the characteristics of stormtroopers.

If the goal of Hitler and the Nazis was to turn Germany's youth into life-long National Socialist supporters and then into soldiers, it was inevitable that the twin planks of youth policy would be the systematic indoctrination and regimentation of German children and adolescents. Accordingly, the Nazis set about changing the nature of everyday life for young Germans.

In Nazi Germany, imbuing children with culture and learning became secondary concerns for the teaching profession. Instead, as a

Above: Hitler Youth protect their ears during the firing of a belt-fed, water-cooled machine gun. Familiarity with different types of weapons prepared young German boys for national service in the *Wehrmacht*.

Right: A typical classroom scene in Germany in the 1930s. To ensure pupils were taught "correctly", all teachers had to attend a month-long training course organized by the Nazi Party.

decree of 18 December 1934 made evident, "the principal task of the school is the education of youth in the service of nationhood and state in the National Socialist spirit". To this end, the Nazis first sought to ensure the political reliability of teachers by "organizing" them into the National Socialist Teachers' League. Following this, the curriculum was re-written to place an emphasis on key aspects of Nazi ideology, thereby turning the classroom into a forum for the subconscious absorption of National

Above: Hitler Youth boys parade their standards. Marching and other outdoor activities were very popular among the Hitler Youth.

Therefore, special attention should be given to the development of the teaching of history." This "special attention" consisted of manipulating the past to make it conform to the Nazi message. German schoolchildren were therefore taught that, throughout the ages, the German people had been superior to all others. Notwithstanding this inherent superiority, deadly and devilish enemies had always threatened the greatness of the German race. In the National Socialist version of history, those enemies bore a striking resemblance to the Nazis' real and imaginary domestic opponents, the communists and the Jews. In this manner, an interpretation of the past was used to justify persecution and oppression in the present.

Past and present heroes

Similarly, the past was also used to elevate Hitler and the Nazi leadership to the status of heroes. According to the new history curriculum, despite the best efforts of Germany's foes, German greatness had always been preserved by the emergence of a national hero who had been able to ward off the danger and lead Germany to new glory. Past heroes included such figures as Charlemagne, Frederick the Great and Bismarck. The present heroes, who had emerged from the chaos of the Weimar years to save Germany from economic and political catastrophe, were Hitler and the National Socialist leadership. The inference to be drawn was that Hitler was the new Charlemagne and the new Frederick.

If the classroom effectively became a venue for political indoctrination, it was by no means the only vehicle for this process. In addition to the school system, another means of promoting the National Socialist message was through the many youth

Left: Baldur von Schirach, the head of the Hitler Youth between 1933 and 1940. He reportedly read *Mein Kampf* in one evening, and his American wife was rumoured to have been at one time a mistress of Hitler.

Socialist ideas. For example, music lessons were used to teach anti-Semitism by making Richard Wagner's essay, *The Jews in Music*, a key classroom text. Similarly, by focusing on stories about fighting and conflict, German language instruction became a vehicle for promoting militarism and a love of war. As one pupil of the time recalled:

A large part of our compulsory reading in German lessons was world war literature … As a rule these were books like "Seven at Verdun" or "Bosemüller Group", in which, amidst all the horrors of modern warfare, the comradeship of the front was still triumphant and if you died you were at least awarded the Iron Cross.

The subject most frequently used to propagate the Nazi message was history. As Minister of the Interior Wilhelm Frick observed in May 1933: "History stands in the foremost place among school subjects.

organizations that the Nazis created
to ensure that the process of
indoctrination continued during
children's leisure time. Most famous
of these bodies was the *Hitler Jugend*
(Hitler Youth or HJ). Almost
immediately after seizing power, the
Nazis created an institutional
structure capable of encompassing all
German children and adolescents.
Headed by the "eternal juvenile"
Baldur von Schirach, who was
appointed Youth Leader of the
German Reich on 17 June 1933, the
system comprised four main
elements. Two associations were
established for girls: the
Jungmädelbund (League of Young
Girls), which covered ages 10 to 14;
and the *Bund Deutscher Mädel*
(League of German Girls),
incorporating girls from 14 to 18.
There were two organizations for

boys: the *Deutsches Jungvolk* (German
Young People), for ages 10 to 14; and
the Hitler Youth itself, for boys aged
14 to 18.

Initially, recruitment to these
groups was on a voluntary basis, with
Schirach proclaiming that "no boy is
to be forced into the Hitler Youth".
However, great efforts were made to
persuade children to join of their own
volition. To this end, rival youth
organizations were progressively
eliminated. The left-wing labour
youth movement was made the subject
of an outright ban, while other
associations were forced to merge with
the Hitler Youth as part of the process
of *Gleichschaltung*. Only the Catholic
youth leagues, which were protected
by an agreement between Hitler and
the Vatican, were able to evade this
process. Even then considerable
pressure was placed upon those

Above: Members of
the *Bund Deutscher
Mädel* at a summer
camp. In the Third
Reich women were
expected to be good
mothers, wives and
Nazis. Women were
specifically excluded
from politics, the
army and the police.

children who joined Catholic youth clubs to enrol in the Hitler Youth instead. It was not unknown for teachers to set extra homework for those pupils who stayed out of the Hitler Youth. If that failed to persuade them, they might be threatened with beatings as well. By such means, the Nazis effectively created a monopoly for themselves in respect of German youth associations. Those children who wanted to take part in such activities had to come to them.

A more positive form of inducement existed in the form of a concerted propaganda campaign designed to emphasize the "new comradeship" provided for the young by the Nazi youth organizations. A prominent example of this phenomenon was the 1933 blockbuster movie *Hitler Youth Quex*. The film was a loose dramatization of the life of 15-year-old Hitler Youth member Herbert Norkus, who had been killed by a gang of communist assailants while distributing Nazi election literature in Berlin during January 1932. The film follows the

fortunes of fictional character Heini Völker. The story, which contains cliché after cliché, is nevertheless very powerful. Heini, the film's hero, comes from a working-class district of Berlin. His father, a life-long communist, is depicted as an alcoholic, a brute and a loafer, who makes the lives of Heini and his mother a misery. She commits suicide in despair, but Heini finds solace as well as comradeship and purpose through joining the Hitler Youth. Such is his commitment to his "new family" that, in protecting his fellow recruits from a communist plot, he dies a martyr's death, proclaiming as he passes away that "the flag means more than death". For the many thousands who saw the film, the message that the Hitler Youth provided comradeship, purpose and a cause worth dying for would have been both apparent and appealing.

The effect of these measures was to make the Nazi youth organizations highly attractive to German children. The historian Stephen Roberts, who visited Nazi Germany in the mid-

Above: German boys, with letters of permission from their parents, queue to enroll in the *Deutsches Jungvolk*. Upon entering each recruit became a "Pimpf" and had to pass mental and physical tests.

1930s and observed the system in operation, noted that "children wanted to join the HJ. To be outside Hitler's organization was the worst form of punishment." As a result, membership grew at an exponential rate. Whereas there had been a mere 108,000 in the Nazi youth movement in December 1932, this had reached 2.2 million by the end of 1933, climbed to 3.6 million by the close of 1934, was just under 4 million in 1935, and hit 5.4 million in 1936. At this point, with rival organizations effectively eliminated and the majority of German youths already integrated within it, a law was passed making participation to all intents and purposes compulsory. This brought the total membership to just over seven million. The incorporation of seven million German young people into one institutional structure gave the Nazis enormous scope to reinforce the programme of indoctrination and regimentation that took place inside Germany's schools. This was a task that the National Socialist youth movements took up with relish.

From the moment children entered the ranks of the German youth movement they were constantly exposed to processes designed to mould them into loyal and obedient servants of the Nazi state. New members of the Hitler Youth were required to swear an oath of allegiance to the Führer. An elaborate induction ceremony was arranged to dignify the occasion and ensure that it was a memorable and impressive event that would instil reverence for the leadership in the young recruit. As one party manual put it: "It is of the greatest importance that the admissions are arranged in a solemn way. For everybody the hour of his induction must be a great experience." Similar ceremonies punctuated a child's progress through the movement, ensuring constant exposure to a message stressing the sanctity and power of the Nazi leadership.

While instilling loyalty to Hitler and the National Socialist state was a key goal of the Nazi youth movement, it was not the only concept that it sought to convey. Another message was the value of *Erlebnis* (experience), especially experience of physical activity. This concept was advanced in various

Below: The hero of the film *Hitler Youth Quex*, watched over by his girlfriend, lies on his bed following a street brawl with communists. The film was very popular in Germany and aided Hitler Youth recruitment.

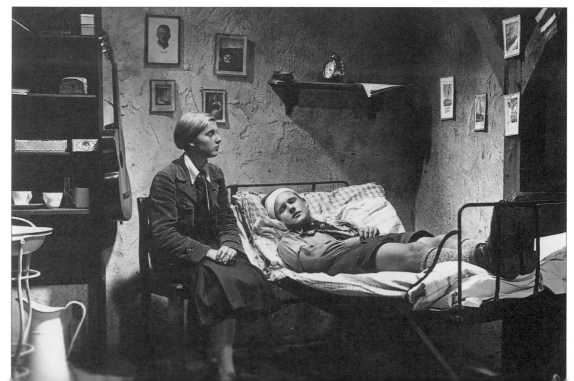

Left: Hitler Youth boys on the rifle range. Weapons training and military exercises were immensely popular among Hitler Youth boys. Using these methods, adolescents could be turned into good Nazis.

Opposite: Morning reveille at a Hitler Youth summer camp at Wörthersee in August 1938. The emphasis on outdoor activities meant Germany's youth was the fittest in Europe by the start of World War II.

Left: The Hitler Youth aimed to develop young boys' latent aggression. Here, young recruits watch a boxing match. Each will take their turn, pairs being matched according to height and weight.

ways. In June 1935, six months' manual labour was made obligatory for German youths in an effort to inculcate the value of hard work and toil among the younger generation. For the most part, the physical activity undertaken under the aegis of the Nazi youth movement took the form of competitive sporting events, including Hitler's favourite, boxing, plus outdoor exercise such as camping and hiking. The purpose of these events was to enhance physical fitness and to promote teamwork and a common cooperative ethos among German children and adolescents. Both of these features were prerequisites of military life, and demonstrate how the activities of the Nazi youth movement were deliberately designed to make the transition from child to soldier that much easier. Neither were these the only features of the Hitler Youth that were geared towards the needs of future military service. The elaborate uniforms, the formal salutes, the drill parades, the flags and ceremonies, and the sub-division of the movement into regional and local branches all gave members of the German youth movement a familiarity with the institutional forms that they would later encounter during national service.

Given the exposure that young Germans had both through the school system and the Nazi youth movement to a systematic programme of indoctrination and regimentation, the question naturally arises: how successful was this in promoting loyalty to the regime and an enthusiasm for martial values among this captive audience of German children and adolescents?

At one level, the answer must be that the success rate was extremely high. The vast majority of young Germans participated in one or more branches of the Nazi youth movement, and many of those who did so embraced its activities with enthusiasm. As Melita Maschmann, a

Below: Baldur von Schirach (centre) shows the Führer a model of the planned Adolf Hitler School, April 1937. The grandiose scheme never reached fruition due to the outbreak of World War II.

Bund Deutscher Mädel official, recorded: "The insatiable thirst which many young people have for action and movement found ample scope in the high-speed action programmes of the Hitler Youth." As a result of such positive experiences, many young Germans embraced wholeheartedly the Nazi Party, promoting its virtues among friends and family. This fact comes across strongly in some of the "Reports on Germany" produced by SOPADE, the German Social Democratic Party in exile. An edition from June 1934 observed that:

...the young people follow the instructions of the HJ and demand from their parents that they become good Nazis, that they give up Marxism, reactionism, and contact with Jews. It is the young men who bring home enthusiasm for the Nazis. Old men no longer make any impression ... the secret of National Socialism is the secret of its youth.

In addition to loyalty, there is plenty of evidence that the system instilled obedience and a martial spirit in Germany's youths. Recalling his experiences of the 1930s, one young German remembered that the constant drills and indoctrination ensured that schoolchildren "were politically programmed: programmed to obey orders, to cultivate the soldierly virtue of standing to attention and saying 'Yes, Sir'...". Unfortunately, this was not the only soldierly trait acquired. As the same memoir goes on to relate, constant exposure to the National Socialist message resulted in young Germans becoming "the willing cannon-fodder of the

Above: Hitler Youth standards on parade, September 1938. Being awarded the special dagger, seen here in the front rank, which bore the motto "Blood and Honour", was a symbol of pride.

National Socialists, softened up for the Second World War".

The achievement of these organizations should not be overstated. Although, for most young Germans, participation in the Nazi youth movement succeeded in promoting loyalty to the regime and in inculcating at least part of the National Socialist message, there was a substantial minority for whom this was not the case. At the margins, there were those who were simply uninterested in the whole scheme and who participated, but purely at a token level. They joined the youth movement only because they had to do so and, once enrolled, conformed to the very minimum extent necessary to avoid attracting notice or incurring punishment. Their very strategy ensured that their apathetic attitude went without notice, thus ensuring no record of their lack of enthusiasm. At the other extreme, there were those who, either because they were alienated by the regimented nature of the Nazi youth movement or because they were simply adverse to authority of any kind, rebelled against the system. Their means of doing this was to reject the Nazi youth sub-culture and set up illicit youth groups of their own, outside the Nazi organization. The trouble that they caused to the authorities ensured that a considerable record of their activities was made.

Among the best known of these alternative youth groups was the *Swing-Jugend* (Swing Kids). Composed largely of young middle-class Germans, often from urban areas, their expression of non-conformity was to reject the regime's preference for "German" music in

Above: Being indoctrinated by Nazi ideology began at a young age. Youths attended "Blood and Soil" events (left) and pageants in honour of the Teutonic Knights at Marienburg (right).

70

favour of an enthusiasm for jazz. As jazz was considered by the Nazis to be tainted by its origins among black communities in the US, this meant the swing youths were acting contrary to National Socialist racial teaching. This was bad enough in peace time, but once the war began and Germany found itself in conflict with Great Britain and America, this preference for the culture of the regime's opponents took on the added stigma of being both "un-German" and unpatriotic. The fact that the swing youths liked to dress in the "English" style, including checked sports jacket and umbrella tucked under the arm, only added to the sense of outrage they caused among the Reich leadership, who advocated taking stringent measures against them. Himmler, for example, called for the swing youth leaders to be sent to concentration camps, where they could be drilled and "given thrashings" until they complied with the rules and norms of the state. As he put it: "In my view … this mischief must be destroyed root and branch. I am against half measures here … It is only by intervening brutally that we shall be able to prevent the dangerous spread of this anglophile tendency."

If a fondness for the jitterbug could land a young German in a concentration camp, then it is hardly surprising that involvement with any of the groups that the Nazis considered actively seditious could

Below: A Nazi nursery rhyme. Even very young children were targets of Nazi ideology – note the flags, uniforms and mock weapons.

Die Fahne hoch! Die Reihen dicht geschlossen,
S.A. marschiert mit mutig festem Schritt.
Kam'raden, die Rotfront und Reaktion erschossen,
Marschier'n im Geist in unsern Reihen mit. Mit Genehmigung der Horst Wessel'schen Erben.

MARBO

Left: Some German youths were active opponents of the Nazis. This is Sophie and Hans Scholl, the leaders of the White Rose resistance group. They were both guillotined in February 1943.

lead to even more drastic punishment. Despite all the pressures towards social and political conformity, several such gangs managed to spring up in working-class areas of Nazi Germany. Included among their number were the *Leipzig Meuten* (packs – which numbered 1500 members), the *Munich Blasen* (crews) and the *Halle Proletengefolgschaften* (proletarian troops). Some of these groups were involved in violent pitched battles with Hitler Youth members. Essentially throwbacks to the former social democratic and communist youth associations, these groups defied the Nazi notion of a *Volksgemeinschaft* by maintaining the primacy of class identities.

More challenging still were the activities of the White Rose group, an organization led by five students from Munich University. Morally opposed to the Nazi regime, whose leadership they described as "beasts" and "criminals", the White Rose produced a series of pamphlets denouncing the Nazis for their tyranny at home, their aggression abroad, and their crimes against humanity in the form of the murder of Jews and Poles. In their second pamphlet they began: "It is

Below: Not all Hitler Youth members were fanatically pro-Nazi. These boys gave themselves up to US troops in Kronach without a fight (April 1945). They watch as their uniforms are burnt in the street.

impossible to come to terms with National Socialism on an intellectual basis, because it is simply not intellectual. You cannot speak of a National Socialist ideology. If such a thing existed, you would be forced to try to defend or engage it on an intellectual basis. Reality offers us a completely different image. When the movement was still in embryonic form, it relied on deception of its fellow man. Even then, it was rotten to the core and could preserve itself only on the basis of constant lies." This was a serious challenge to the regime which reacted, after capturing the group, by torturing and then beheading them.

Equally problematic for the regime were the various groups known collectively as the Edelweiss Pirates. Named after the edelweiss flower badges they wore on the collars of their invariably colourful clothing, they consisted of young people who were not only opposed to the authoritarian and hierarchical nature of the Nazi youth organizations, but were actually willing to risk taking action against them. In addition to the usual acts of protest, involving gathering together outside the confines of the Hitler Youth to enjoy "un-German" music and dancing, the Edelweiss Pirates also composed anti-Nazi songs, wrote anti-Nazi slogans as graffiti across Germany's cities, and even deliberately sought out fights with those who conformed with the Nazi system, especially members of the Hitler Youth. The appearance of slogans such as "Down with Hitler" on the walls of Düsseldorf's pedestrian subways and assaults on Hitler Youth members represented real, if ultimately ineffectual, challenges to the authority of the National Socialist state, and were events that the regime could not tolerate. Determined action was taken by the *Gestapo* to find and apprehend the group's ringleaders. Those whom they caught were dealt with severely. For example, in November 1944 several members of the Cologne Edelweiss Pirates, one only 16, were hanged publicly.

These executions represent the ultimate testimony of Nazi youth policies. The goal of the regime was to transform Germany's youth into Nazi Party loyalists and willing soldiers. Those who got caught up in the spell of the regime's elaborate indoctrination programme ultimately gained little but the chance to die on the battlefield. Those who resisted risked persecution and death at home. In the end, therefore, Nazi youth policies were little more than a sacrifice of youth on a grand scale.

Below: Hitler Youth captured in Berlin in May 1945. These are the lucky ones. Thousands of young boys died in Germany in 1945 trying to stop the advance of the Allied armies, especially the dreaded Russians.

Chapter 5
Women

National Socialism excluded women from politics, from the armed forces and from the legal profession. The party saw a woman's role as being a good mother, wife and Nazi supporter, summed up in their phrase "children, church and kitchen".

Nazi ideas often grew from what they considered to be incontestable truths of nature. Attitudes to others in society were deemed to be based on the biological bedrock of racial identity, making Jews, gypsies and Slavs (described by the Nazis as "chaff") less than equal to Aryan Germans. Similarly, attitudes to gender were based on what they considered to be equally rigid natural laws. It wasn't surprising, therefore, to hear Adolf Hitler say in a speech of 1934 to a Nazi women's organization that: "We do not consider it correct for the woman to interfere in the world of man, in his main sphere. We consider it natural if these two worlds remain distinct."

It seems little more than a reiteration of the classic argument of the two spheres: the public, political sphere is the male domain; the private, domestic sphere is that of woman. This was a language any mid-nineteenth man could embrace. In essence it was deeply conservative. It was this conservatism that made Nazi attitudes to women attractive well beyond usual pro-Nazi circles. Their ideas and policies on sex, marriage and the family appealed profoundly to German Catholics, whether as individuals or as an organized group such as the church. Among the ex-soldiers, so numerous in the early Nazi Party, and the SA, who sought a recreation of the all-male camaraderie of the trenches,

Below: German soldiers in a dugout in World War I. After the war many ex-soldiers who became Nazi Party members sought to recreate the all-male camaraderie of the trenches – women were excluded.

such male chauvinistic attitudes were, not surprisingly, common. Women were effectively excluded from Nazi activities before 1933.

Those attitudes were reinforced by Nazi opposition to the democratic ambitions of Weimar Germany, which ensured universal female suffrage and created educational and work opportunities for women on an unprecedented scale. To the marginalized disgruntled early Nazi, the image of "the modern woman" became an object of hate. This was a complex combination of the "blue stocking" (educated woman); the woman in paid industrial employment who neglected her husband and family; the woman wearing trousers and smoking; the woman who might be a prostitute or even a lesbian; and the woman who demanded rights but neglected her domestic duties. Not surprisingly, Hitler went on to say in the 1934 speech: "The slogan 'Emancipation of women' was invented by Jewish intellectuals." A graver indictment of the failure of true German womanliness could not be imagined than this, direct from the Führer's own mouth.

Nazi attitudes to women

When the Nazis came to power, their attitudes to women were fundamentally anti-feminist, anti-liberal and remarkably paternalistic. Just as they rejected Weimar democracy with its notions of equality, so they rejected what they thought was the inappropriate role and status of women. Instead, they offered another, "truer" role for women. Hitler's 1934 speech stated: "What the man gives in courage on the battlefield, the woman gives in eternal self-sacrifice, in eternal pain and suffering. Every child that a woman brings into the world is a battle, a battle waged for the existence of her people."

This brings us to a central aspect of Nazi policies towards women. One of the key demands of Hitler and the Nazis from 1933 onwards was for a dramatic increase in the birthrate. Hitler, Himmler and many other Nazis were obsessed with a sense of Germany's decline. One manifestation of this was its dwindling birthrate and the sense

Above: Though revered, women were seen only as breeding machines.

Below: Large families were encouraged by Hitler, to boost the German population.

that, in the long run, Germany's recovery as a power would be thwarted by existing in an ever-rising tide of prolifically multiplying Slavs. Decadent Weimar society, they alleged, had allowed the one- or two-child German family to develop. This was not a sufficient basis for a re-emergent Germany seeking to dominate Europe. While extreme Nationalists and Nazis might present this as a uniquely German problem, it was a more common West European problem after 1918 as increasingly urbanized populations reduced the number of children they had in order to raise their standards of living and comfort. It was as bad in France and even worse in Austria. Nazi attitudes and policies didn't allow them to make a more rational assessment.

The quest for more children

The Nazis tended to view the German woman, despite the concealing verbiage of "motherhood", essentially as a unit of reproduction. "The *volkisch* community expected women in the new Germany to become mothers, indeed it was a duty imposed upon them by nature." Consequently, to prevent the obstacles that Weimar had allegedly placed in the way of conception and childbirth, the Nazis enforced anti-abortion legislation zealously. Between 1934 and 1938, there was a 50 percent increase in convictions. They also closed birth-control clinics and placed every obstacle in the way of the propagation and distribution of contraceptive devices, practices and knowledge. These were policies supported and endorsed by the Catholic church in Germany.

In addition, incentives were offered that sought to further conception and encourage more children to be born in wedlock. One of these was the Marriage Loan, part of a programme introduced in June

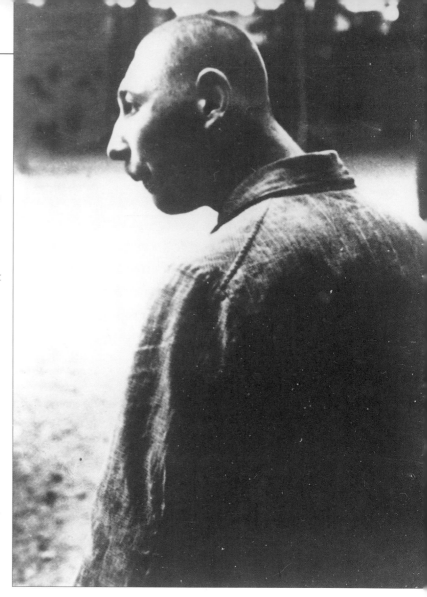

Above: Though Hitler promoted the rapid growth of the German population, he only wanted pure Aryan bloodstock. Non-Aryans, as well as the disabled and mentally ill (as here), had no place in the Third Reich.

Left: Medals such as the Mother's Cross were awarded to women with very large families.

1933 as a "Law for the Promotion of Marriage". The loan was intended to encourage couples to marry and produce children. It was interest free, and was to be paid back over a 100-month period at one percent per month. The loans averaged RM600 (roughly equivalent to four months of an average industrial wage). The sum to be repaid was subsequently cut by 25 percent for each child produced. Up to 1937, approximately a third of all couples marrying received such a loan, some 700,000 in all. Other devices available included maternity benefits with extra income tax allowances for dependent children, financed by imposing increased taxes on single people and childless couples. While these measures may have had some immediate effect on encouraging marriages, they did not have the desired effect on the population. Marriages increased from 630,000 in 1933 to 740,200 in 1934, but the birthrate did not rise correspondingly. Live births in 1933 were 971,174; a year later they were 1,198,350. With about 750,000 deaths per year, the net population increase was only 450,000. It was only in 1938 and 1939 that it exceeded 500,000.

The much vaunted and trumpeted *Geburtenschlacht* (battle for births) did not seem to be a victorious campaign, despite the well-publicized bronze, silver and gold medals issued to dutifully prolific females who had six or more children. Most women seemed to prefer to have one or two children. Indeed, there were reports in the late 1930s of some one million women still single as well as 5.4 million women still childless. This was despite Himmler's little homily, "Only he who leaves a child behind can die with equanimity". Clearly not all German women were listening, let alone responding. There was probably an extremely practical reason for this. The growth of the Nazi economy, with its particular emphasis on rearmament and preparation for war, did not provide a significant house-building programme. Lack of space and lack of money perhaps determined women's responses to the Nazi drive for procreation.

This battle for births had, like all Nazi campaigns, an ominously negative side. Only appropriate women, the truly Aryan, were encouraged and expected to have offspring prolifically. The fear was that Jews, gypsies, the disabled, those suffering from hereditary illnesses,

Below: Men had traditionally toiled the land, but as urban industry increased, they went to work in the factories, leaving the women to work on the farms.

the presumed "a-socials", would breed and thus degrade German bloodstock. Horrific images of a rising tide of these "undesirables", deemed to be a burden on Nazi progress, were frequently shown in propaganda sources and documentary films. The aim was to make actions that were being considered against such people more widely acceptable to the German public. One measure was the introduction of compulsory sterilization in 1933, which resulted in more than 300,000 German citizens being compelled to undergo surgery to prevent the possibility of them adding to "the burden". While this measure applied to both men and women, it was indicative of Nazi attitudes to women and procreation. They were not having children for their own or their family's sake but in order to provide future *Volksgenossen* (national comrades). Consequently, they had a role to ensure the appropriate upbringing, such as membership of the Hitler Youth.

Above: At the Rendsburg Agricultural School, women farm hands learn how to milk a cow. Women became increasingly important in the running of farmland during the Nazi years in power.

Left: The traditional role of women as a *haus frau* or housewife providing for the family was a strong Nazi ideal.

Failure to bring children up in the approved manner could, in extreme cases, result in the child or children being transferred to a state institution.

There was a slightly more benign aspect to this policy. The National

Socialist Welfare Organization (*National Sozialistische Volkswohlfahrt* – NSV) helped to organize and run "Mother and Child" programmes. These offered, beyond the unavoidable ideological indoctrination of being a Nazi woman and mother, housekeeping classes and motherhood skills in some 25,000 advice centres. These were used, it was claimed, by some 10 million women. A flavour of the ideological input is given in the "Ten Commandments for the choice of a spouse":

1. Remember that you are a German.
2. If you are genetically healthy you should not remain unmarried.
3. Keep your body pure.
4. You should keep your mind and spirit pure.
5. As a German choose only a spouse of the same or Nordic blood.
6. In choosing a spouse ask about his ancestors.
7. Health is also a precondition for physical beauty.
8. Marry only for love.
9. Don't look for a playmate but for a companion for marriage.
10. You should want to have as many children as possible.

The other major Nazi approach to women, beyond that of biological reproduction, was that of their place in the economy, their vital role as "producers". As the chapter on the economy will show, initial Nazi concerns in 1933 were centred on the "battle for jobs". This was to have a major effect on women.

In the Weimar period and continuing into the years of the depression, female employment in the German industrial economy had followed the normal pattern of a modern, industrializing and urbanizing society. More and more women left the domestic sphere, or traditional family employment on farms or in small shops. This was magnified by the after-effects of

World War I as Germany had approximately two million more women than men. There were around 500,000 more widows in the 1920s than before the war. Necessity as much as desire drove more women into the labour market, so much so that some 11.5 million women were defined as "economically active" in 1925. Of these, more than four million were in regular paid employment outside family farms or businesses. They became part of a diversified workforce in industry, commerce and the bureaucracies of central and local government agencies. Their roles were as typists and secretaries, shop assistants, doctors, teachers, nurses, film stars, actresses and musicians. Many more were taking advantage of the increased opportunities for higher and university education that Weimar offered. All of these developments were seen as ideologically pernicious by the incoming Nazi regime. A woman's place was in the home, the famous slogan of the three Ks (in German, the kindergarten, the kitchen and the church). If not directly in the home, work should be on the family peasant farm or in the corner shop, both so beloved of *Mittelstand* (petty bourgeois) Germany and its traditional conservative views of women's roles and place.

Women in industry

Women in paid employment were frequently stigmatised as *Doppleverdiener* (second income earners) or, in slang, double dippers. The blithe assumption was that it was somehow a luxury that could be dispensed with. This was perhaps understandable in 1932 and 1933, with male unemployment at 29 percent (female unemployment was approximately 11 percent). The Nazi drive to reverse this was not only a central part of their "battle for jobs", but was widely appreciated in male circles. Popular male images of women coincided closely with Nazi propaganda. Domestic work was seen as the norm. If paid work was done it should be what the Nazis deemed "intrinsically female", such as welfare work and teaching. To ensure that "womanly work" was undertaken, as well as to create more jobs for men,

Below: German women working in a munitions factory during the war. As almost all fit and healthy men were called up to fight, the women were left to support Germany's war effort.

women were removed from paid urban employment through a variety of devices. Exhortation, official encouragement and advice to labour exchanges to discriminate against women were significant and carried a good measure of public support. More directly, women in official organizations could and would be sacked by the now Nazified authorities. The marriage loans scheme fitted in with this policy, as the borrowers agreed that "the future wife pledges herself not to take up employment so long as her future husband receives an income of more than RM125 a month".

We can see Nazi attitudes to women as "producers" coinciding with their view of them as "reproducers". If the women were placed in the home, then the expectation was that they were more likely to conceive. This attitude is revealed more fully in a contemporary popular official pamphlet which sought to remind "national comrades":

Sexual activity serves the purpose of procreation for the maintenance of the life of the nation and not for the enjoyment of the individual. If, however, the desire to have a child has been fulfilled and the continuation and enlargement of the nation has been secured by the production of a sufficient number of children, then, from the point of view of the nation, there is no objection to further satisfaction of the sexual urge.

Against the background of the recovery of the German economy from 1933 to 1936, the increase in the level of female employment, from 4.85 million to 5.36 million, was not dramatic. While the numbers increased, the percentage of women in the workforce declined from 29.3 percent to 24.7 percent. By 1938 it

Above: Collecting peat from Emsland Moor, young German women do their bit for the war effort. Pressed into serving for one year, they would have received no pay for their efforts.

stood at only 25 percent. The Nazis might seek to claim some credit for this, but the situation developed less out of their attitude to women and employment than out of their need to develop the capital goods sector and the general transport infrastructure. The beginning of rearmament, which needed male labourers, led to rapid expansion; while the neglected domestic consumer goods and services sectors, with more women workers, expanded very slowly. Male unemployment therefore fell dramatically without, simultaneously, drawing large numbers of women into paid work.

The demand for female labour

This coincidence between Nazi ideology towards women and the practical demands of the economy was to come increasingly into conflict from 1936 onwards. The Four Year Plan, the drive for rearmament and autarky (self-sufficiency) led not only to full employment but also to a mounting demand for more and more labour. Ultimately, only increased female labour could meet this demand. So the "primacy of economics" seemed to be triumphing over the "primacy of biology". As we shall see, it was to be only a partial victory for political necessity over ideological rigidity.

As the economy heated up and the demand for female labour grew more intense between 1936 and 1939, the Nazis had to make adjustments. In part this came from an increasing move of labour from the rural sector. This involved primarily, but not exclusively, younger men moving into the industrial workforce. One Nazi response to this was the introduction of Labour Service for Girls. At first, in 1936, it was voluntary. But with a paltry take-up of some 1000 volunteers, it was transformed in January 1939 into a one-year service obligation, with the "girls" pressed

into unpaid farm work and household and domestic service.

The demand for female labour mounted again in 1939 with increased male military conscription. In the war years, with military losses and the increasing moves to a "Total War" economy, it continued to increase. The Nazis still held back from a full mobilization of the reserve army of "women", despite the efforts of Hermann Göring and Albert Speer to get more women into munitions production. In 1939, approximately 14.6 million women were in the economy. By September 1944, this had risen to 14.9 million (before dipping to 14.1 million in 1941). In this respect the Nazi regime was far less successful than wartime Great Britain, which moved in 1941 to introduce compulsion and subscription. Nazi Germany was less

Above: The cover of *The Week* magazine, depicting a wholesome Aryan German girl working the land. Propaganda extolling the virtues of female labour were abundant in Nazi Germany, especially after 1939.

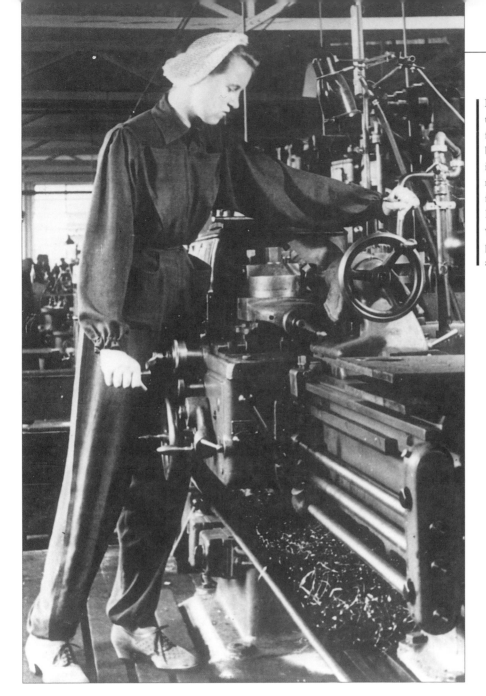

Left: In addition to working on farmland, women became increasingly involved in hard manual labour in factories. As in Great Britain, it was the women who produced the tanks, aircraft and bullets.

successful, despite the 1943 decree that all women between 17 and 45 be conscripted. This was then extended to women up to 50. However, it resulted in a net increase of only some 500,000 women mobilized. This was in spite of the 1 million single women and 5.4 million childless women referred to earlier. Part of the explanation lies in Nazi prejudices about women and the crude stereotypes they had fostered. These 1943 measures were not only limited because of the plethora of

exemptions allowed; they were also immensely unpopular, which meant that more and more women sought exemption. Therefore, Germany's reserve army of labour came instead from foreign workers and virtual slave labourers (women as well as men), some seven million of them by 1945, dragged from all corners of the Nazi empire.

Nazi attitudes always countenanced and encouraged female work in agriculture. A mixture of conservative ideological nostalgia

83

coupled with dubious ideas of "'blood and soil" created a propagandistic image of women's rural work as somehow natural and becoming. Blonde-haired young women in traditional peasant costumes against golden wheat fields bathed in sun smiled out from Nazi propaganda posters. They were but another strand of Nazi mythology. In truth, women made up half the agricultural workforce. They were particularly concentrated in the smaller peasant farms that Nazi ideology had so extolled as a part of the traditional backbone of a wholesome regenerated Reich. In fact, this was a desperately exploited workforce, and no amount of propagandistic praise could lift from them the crushing burden of unmechanized toil. However, they were absolutely central to German agricultural production, especially as Germany from 1933 onwards strove to reduce imports in its search for economic self-sufficiency.

Of these women who made up half of the peacetime agricultural labour force, three-quarters were not hired or paid employees, but family members for whom labour was a barely escapable duty. On the smallest farms, under 2 hectares (4.9 acres), women constituted 70 percent of the labour force. The sheer extent of this exploited labour was revealed in a 1939 study which recorded that a woman's work year in agriculture consisted of 3933 hours, about 10.75 hours every day for 365 days. The same study recorded male hours as 3544, and contrasted that with figures of 2400 to 2700 for industrial employment. Even Goebbels' propaganda efforts could not possibly disguise the reality from the people who endured it. And this takes no account of the classic "double burden" of women with domestic household responsibilities of food preparation, cleaning and child-rearing. Little wonder that Nazi

Below left: Female students in Weimar Berlin. Independent women did not fit the Nazi ideal.

Below right: At the Randsburg Agricultural School, young women were taught rifle shooting.

attitudes to women and domesticity had a ready reception among male peasant farmers. Many of these had been early recruits to the Nazi movement in the agricultural depression of 1928. It was equally unsurprising that peasant women, especially the younger ones, saw the potential lure of the cities and paid urban work. They were not likely to accept Nazi strictures against it.

The League of German Girls

A survey conducted by a Hitler Youth leader among girls between 10 and 14 in his district recorded that all save one reported that they wanted to go to the city. He scornfully recorded his own view that this was merely a response to "cinemas, fashionable clothes and the other attractions of the big city". Without any evidence to support it, there is the distinct feeling that the one girl who did not want to go to the city was this youth leader's own daughter.

For rural women in Nazi Germany it would seem that the League of German Girls offered little in the way of a counter-attraction to the presumed and desired bright lights. Reactionary propaganda and images clearly did not satisfy these young girls. However, the organizational practices, camps and visits did at least open horizons and offer a glimpse of

alternatives, albeit briefly, far from the confines of home and family. Such desires could only be satisfied by a permanent move away from the countryside, which would have left the farms even more short-handed.

Not only were rural women expected to fulfil Nazi "production" norms, they were also under pressure to achieve the pro-nationalist "reproduction" norms. It is not surprising, therefore, that infant mortality rates were consistently higher in rural areas. In Pomerania and Bavaria infant deaths were more common than in Berlin. Even inner cities in a modern industrializing society were better for child-rearing and child-bearing than the Nazis' mythologized countryside.

The issue of women in Nazi Germany has been a subject of debate and discussion among historians over several generations, without a consensus emerging. Some have seen this period as one of fairly unrelieved male chauvinism. Women were excluded from full membership of the Nazi Party. There were no women members of the *Reichstag* after 1933. Unrelenting images of motherhood and domesticity, accompanied by restricted employment opportunities, were the norm. These included Hitler's arbitrary prohibition on any woman holding any significant legal

Left Mother's Day in Berlin, 1942. The elderly lady sitting down has just been awarded the Mother's Cross, and is handed a bouquet of flowers by a young member of the League of German Girls.

position. Not surprisingly, these historians view the Nazis as essentially an anti-feminist regime seeking to impose reactionary work and conservative nationalist policies which would severely handicap women and utterly prevent them from playing a full role in society.

Others have argued that there is a discrepancy between Nazi intentions and the actual consequences of their policies in action. They point to the increase in the number of women in paid industrial employment; to their extended employment in the chemical, electrical and rubber industries; and to some increase by 1945 of women in higher education. Initially, the Nazis sought to operate a quota system for women's entrance to universities, setting it at 10 percent in 1933 (or 1500 places out of 10,000 eligible). After 1939 the figure rose to 20 percent and above. These and comparable changes are seen as the Nazis unwittingly presiding over a social revolution (albeit a different one to the one they aimed for) which raised the status and opportunities of women despite their ideological hostilities to female progress beyond their narrow, predetermined stereotypes. The claim is made that their intended conservative revolution failed, and instead they produced for women "a new status of relative if unconventional equality". Given some of the points made in this chapter, that is a hard concept to accept.

From a more modern standpoint in terms of female emancipation, this

Left: A "dutiful" mother salutes Hitler's cavalcade as her young daughter looks on.

Below: As part of the effort to ease the burden of wartime shortages, women were encouraged to swap unwanted items at special exchanges like the one below.

was clearly something the Nazis resolutely and consistently opposed in a fundamentally and biologically justified way. Their unshakeable conviction in the immutability of racial and biological differences remained constant. Just as they regarded "races" as distinct and separate, so they regarded men and women as different. The difference implied that just as the Führer led the party in a way not open to challenge, so man the political animal was destined by nature to lead woman, the domestic one. Only as a result would men and women achieve their true natural capabilities.

The failure of Nazi policy

Economic contingencies forced the Nazis in some respects to trim and adjust policy, especially in relation to female labour in industry. This may have increased the opportunities for some women beyond those that their male rulers had contemplated or intended. This simply meant, however, that the restrictions imposed were not as savage as initially aimed for. This is hardly a definition of progress or beneficial change.

Given the racial and biological determinants of so much of Nazi policy here as elsewhere, the opportunities were circumscribed in terms of those arbitrarily drawn boundaries which so often stemmed from Hitler's dogmatic utterances. This was especially so for all those women who suffered under Nazi tyranny: Jewish women; Aryan women married to Jews; gypsy women; women and girls classified as "life unworthy of life" and murdered; women and girls considered biologically unfit to have children and compulsorily sterilized; foreign women turned into slave workers or prostitutes; peasant women treated as little better than breeders and beasts of burden – the list rolls on.

Even Aryan women, the "chosen" of this regime, were not granted the autonomy to exert full biological control over their own bodies, or over their intellectual and economic capabilities. Nevertheless, the Nazis did not fully realize their ideological goals of treating women purely as "producers" or "reproducers", and had to settle for an aborted outcome. These "reactionary modernizers" ultimately failed.

Below: Women collectors for "Winter Aid" with Adolf Hitler on the day of National Solidarity in 1937.

Chapter 6
Urban life and country life

The success of Nazi economic policies boosted urban employment and the living standards of ordinary urban Germans. In the countryside, however, notwithstanding government policies, the living standards of rural workers were poor by comparison.

The town and country were worlds apart during the time of the Third Reich. From 1933 Nazi economic policy effectively rejuvenated urban living. The policies of massive public works schemes, rearmament and autarky ("self-sufficiency", acquiring essential raw materials from domestic production rather than imports) favoured the industrial base concentrated in towns and cities. Conversely, the rural community withered and struggled, shedding workers for city employment and declining through a mixture of debt, poor wages and under-investment.

Urban business

Urban areas were the primary beneficiaries of the huge drop in unemployment in Nazi Germany between 1933 in 1939, from six million to only 309,000 in just six years. Despite government countermeasures, many of the new urban workers came from a massive exodus of disadvantaged agricultural labourers hoping to join the boom in city employment. Between 1925 and 1939, the German employed population in total increased by 10.6

Left: A propaganda poster for the *Deutsche Arbeitsfront* (German Labour Front). The front was in effect the sole labour organization of the Third Reich, setting wage levels and settling any industrial disputes.

percent. The workforce in industry grew by 7 percent, within trade and transport by 14 per cent, and in service industries by a huge 67 percent. By stark contrast the agricultural and forestry workforce contracted by nearly 9 percent in the same period, and from 1934 to 1939 1.5 million agricultural workers deserted the land for the city.

Germany's towns and cities were undoubtedly hosts to tremendous commercial growth during the Nazi period, hence their rapacious need for workers. On the whole it was a good time to run a business (as long as you weren't Jewish). The general rule for businesses in the Third Reich was that the bigger you were, the more you had to benefit from the Nazi regime. In the late 1920s most big businesses had been hostile to the Nazi Party. Hitler's politics contained the nationalism and militarism feared by industry and commerce, which had already experienced the financial destruction of World War I only a few years previously.

Yet as Hitler took power in 1933, the view changed. Large industrial concerns such as the Krupp and Thyssen engineering and steel companies benefited from Hitler's abolishment of troublesome trade unions and their replacement with the business-friendly *Deutsche Arbeitsfront* (DAF). Huge government contracts brought profits to the building, armaments, chemicals and metal industries, leading to production increases in industrial goods of over 100 percent between 1932 and 1939. The Nazis also capped wages for workers at 1929 Depression levels to beat inflation, and increased control of labour allocation. For businesses this meant workers became less expensive and less able to transfer their labour to other companies.

Large city businesses also managed to increase profit even after the war began. Conquered territories provided a vast army of slave labour requiring no wages, no benefits and little company outlay. In 1939, 266,000 foreign labourers (foreign civilians and POWs) were working within Germany in non-agricultural roles, 0.6 percent of the urban/industrial workforce. By 1944, 4,724,000 foreigners were working (in the sense of being forced labour)

Above: The metallurgical industry benefited from Nazi contracts in the 1930s.

Below: A somewhat romanticized image of East European workers in Germany in World War II.

in urban Germany, 22 percent of the entire non-agricultural workforce. The benefits to German businesses from this large reservoir of free labour must have been marked, salaries being the greatest output of many commercial enterprises.

Of course, foreign labourers were not the only disadvantaged group to benefit businesses in urban Germany. Measures against Jewish business owners steadily pushed them out of the economy altogether. In April 1938 all Jewish assets over RM5000 had to be registered, with the government channelling these assets into industries of its choosing. This policy drove almost every Jewish business into liquidation. The destruction or "Aryanization" of Jewish businesses significantly reduced competition for many other German concerns. Small, medium-sized businesses in urban retail and craft sectors were initial profiteers, as competing Jewish shops and department stores were closed down or appropriated. Larger corporations also enjoyed the move, acquiring numerous Jewish enterprises and taking over the Jewish share of the consumer-goods market. Most Jewish businesses, however, were simply shut down rather than taken over. As Richard Grunberger has pointed out (*A Social History of the Third Reich*,

Above: Nazi economic policy in action. The SA and SS enforce a boycott of Jewish businesses in Berlin in April 1933. Most Jewish businesses were shut down or driven into bankruptcy by the Nazi regime.

Weidenfeld & Nicholson, 1971), only 700 of the 3750 Jewish shops owned at the time of *Kristallnacht* (November 1938) were appropriated by other businesses.

While non-Jewish urban businesses were beneficiaries of many Nazi policies, there were negatives. Entrepreneurial handling of a business was effectively quashed under centralized Nazi control. Subservience to huge state contracts meant that many businesses were forced to have Nazi military or civil service personnel on the boards of directors. More and more sectors of industry were either run directly by the state or by state-supported monopolies – a full 70 percent of Germany's industrial production was in the hands of monopolies in 1937. Any business, regardless of size, was ultimately subservient to government. In 1933, steel industry giants such as United Steel Works, Krupp and Mannesmann refused to begin the large-scale production of low-quality ores as part of the autarky programme. As punishment, Hermann Göring founded the modestly named state producer *Reichswerke Hermann Göring*. The

government took 70 percent of the new corporation's capital, and had priority claim over any available labour, raw materials or technology in the German workplace. To add insult to injury, the government forced the big steel companies to buy the corporation's remaining shares at a cost of RM130 million. From this point onwards, the government effectively controlled all German steel production.

Small businesses were also far from immune to Nazi interference. Reams of Nazi legislation restricted the open trade and light

Above: Building up Germany's military might: a steam locomotive hauls a heavy block of iron along a track at the Krupp steel works.

Below: This is the Krupp works at Essen, scene of frenetic activity as the Nazis geared up for war in Europe.

administration so essential to a smooth-running small business. Tax collection and financial procedures were ruthlessly monitored, and from 1935 all businesses were required to keep and present accounts. The Nazis essentially did not value small businesses, seeing them as diffusing the government streamlining of industry. Consequently, many small businesses were forced into cartels (radio retailers, for example, had their numbers halved between 1933 and 1939) or simply pushed out of business by legislation (over 168,000 between 1936 and 1940). The creation of new shops and businesses required official permission from local government, a notoriously slow bureaucracy. But in the face of such obtrusive forces, German businesses still managed to create employment for the masses.

Although poverty remained prevalent during the entire tenure of the Third Reich, full employment gave the cities a prosperous feel. White-collar urban professionals rose in numbers as the government created thousands of new positions in city administration. In 1933, for example, there were roughly 5.5 million civil servants in Germany. Professional workers helped maintain Germany's urban restaurant culture, which thrived on the fact that restaurants and cafes could maintain culinary standards through plentiful non-rationed foodstuffs such as fish and game.

Combined with a working class who were, if not wealthy, at least solvent, the cities enjoyed reasonable buoyancy in the consumption of leisure and entertainment services and consumer goods. Alcohol and coffee intake increased; wine drinking by 50 percent between 1933 and 1938. The consumption of almost all foodstuffs rose, apart from when war rationing bit from 1939. Those items not available through legal purchase were usually accessible through the black market. The holiday programmes offered by the *Kraft durch Freude* (KdF; Strength through Joy) accounted for roughly one week's wage each year among working-class households. Cinema going also increased, especially

Above: A Nazi "Strength through Joy" gymnastics event in Wannsee, Berlin, held on 24 April 1937.

Opposite top: Public holidays in the Third Reich were packed with events, such as this mass rally at Nuremberg.

Opposite bottom: A Nazi winter festival, March 1936. Such events stressed the relationship between rural workers and the soil.

during the war when the public craved campaign news and, later, escapism. Attendance at Germany's 7000 cinemas, for example, went up by around 80 percent just in the first year of the war.

Public holidays

Entertainment for the urban masses also came in the form of numerous public holidays and Nazi festivals. By 1938 there were 11 major Nazi festivals or holidays (religious holidays were basically dropped or replaced). These included Day of the Seizure of Power (30 January), Hitler's Birthday (20 April), Day of the Summer Solstice, the Reich Party Rally at Nuremberg (September) and the Anniversary of the 1923 Beer Hall *Putsch* (9 November). It was not in the Nazis' nature to simply allow people to use these holidays as free time. Instead they were packed with events, parties, rallies and gatherings which reinforced Nazi propaganda. For example, Hitler's Birthday transformed cities and towns across Germany. Almost every home placed photographs of the Führer in the windows and hung out red, white and black bunting from their houses. At night, vast torchlight parades lit

up the streets, stadiums and conference halls.

Such events added genuine colour to the lives of Germany's urban population, but could not always obscure gloom in other areas of city living. Although it is commonly said that Hitler "made the buses run on time", other amenities were not so lucky. City hospitals found themselves deprived of expert medical personnel through a curious quirk in Nazi priorities. On coming to power the Nazis cut the length of medical training by two years. The result was a 40 percent drop in specialist doctors, compounded by the expulsion of 5500 Jewish doctors from the medical profession. Furthermore, many qualified doctors went into military, government or private health practice after graduation, further starving city hospitals of expertise. These factors resulted in a drop of six percent in the doctor-to-patient ratio over six years.

At the same time as the Nazis were cutting the length of medical

training, they were also slashing the university population in general. Prior to the rise of National Socialism, Germany had prided itself on a vibrant intellectual and liberal culture within its cities and towns. The Nazi regime was radically anti-intellectual, and this had a purging effect on urban cultural institutions, particularly libraries and universities. On 10 May 1933 a huge gathering of party members, Hitler Youth and Nazi students across Germany raided public and private libraries and stripped them of books written by Jewish authors or other "politically undesirable" writers. In Berlin, the books were thrown into a huge pile opposite the university on the Unter der Linden and burnt. The thousands of volumes destroyed included works by Karl Marx, Erich Maria Remarque, Marcel Proust, H.G. Wells, Jack London and Sigmund Freud.

This event symbolized the Nazis' new antipathy towards academic pursuits. Germany in 1932 contained some of the finest universities in the

Above: German students and Nazi paramilitary members burning "un-German" books in Berlin in May 1933. In total, as a band played, 20,000 books were destroyed in Berlin city centre alone.

Western world, but they soon suffered under Nazi policy. In 1932 there were 127,580 students in higher education. By 1934 this figure had fallen to 92,622 and kept falling until 1941, when it reached an all-time low of 40,968.

The enforcement of Nazi ideology wrecked academic standards. All Jewish and dissenting academic staff were dismissed from their posts, around 10 percent of university teachers. With typical Nazi blindness, the expulsions focused on many of Germany's most eminent academics, resulting in the intellectual collapse of entire departments. The academics left were constantly scrutinized by Third Reich officials or Nazi colleagues. They had their work contracts set by government officers, and also had to attend a six-week Lecturer's Association Camp. Here they underwent political indoctrination and physical tests, and passing the camp satisfactorily became a condition of academic employment. Many lecturers decided it was too much, and quit for the easier option of working in better paid and more prestigious industry positions. The universities left behind were shadows of their former selves. Academic standards plummeted, and

the curriculum filled up with Nazi-style military and technical courses.

Later on the Nazi Party realized its anti-intellectualism was self-defeating. Deficient educations limited the contributions young people could make to the state, especially in militarily vital fields such as technology and engineering. From 1937 the number of industry sponsored science and engineering scholarships were increased, but only enough to raise the number of funded students to around two percent of the total university/technical college population. Other students usually had to pay their own way, not easy when total of outlay for a university course, including living expenses, could be more than 10,000 marks.

Above: Enforcing Nazi ideology. Berlin students march on the Institute for Sexual Science prior to closing it down for being a "haven of Jewish science".

Below: A solemn procession of students, bearing torches and swastika banners, 19 May 1933. They are about to make a bonfire of works considered to be "contrary to the German spirit".

No surprise, therefore, that around 95 percent of university students were from well off middle-class or upper-class homes. In 1939 only 3.5 percent of college students were working class.

Nazi architecture and housing

The most visible evidence of the Nazi regime in the towns and cities was architectural. For all Hitler's anti-intellectualism, architecture remained an abiding and passionate interest. His sketchbooks as a teenager and young adult in Vienna were crammed with formidable neo-baroque architectural structures such as the Vienna Opera House. Even prior to 1933, Hitler understood that public architecture would be a vital statement of the Nazi regime's philosophy and power, a permanent working act of propaganda. Stylistically, Hitler lent towards the gravitas of classical Greek or Roman architecture and the ornamentation of Renaissance palaces and baroque castles – all forms which combined scale, authority and connotations of imperial destiny.

Adapting the past styles to present Nazi mythology fell to a few select architects. Paul Ludwig Troost was one of the first to turn Hitler's architectural dreams into stone. Troost began working for the Nazis in the late 1920s, and in 1930 Hitler gave him the job of transforming the Barlow Palace in Munich into the new Nazi Party headquarters. He accomplished the job for a total investment of RM800,000 (most supplied in a loan to the Nazi Party from the Thyssen industrial concern). Hitler was delighted with the result, and Troost became Hitler's favourite architect. Troost subsequently refurnished the Chancellery residency in Berlin.

Below: The *Haus der Deutschen Kunst* (House of German Art) was one of Hitler's first building projects. The museum was designed by Paul Ludwig Troost, who did not live to see its opening in 1937.

96

From 1933, Germany's urban citizens noticed an explosion of public building construction. Almost every town and city received new neo-classical buildings serving political, administrative or legal government functions. Troost created a new House of German Art in Munich. The pediments of party headquarters attracted monumental Greco-Roman nude sculptures from the likes of Josef Thorak, who also created a huge *Autobahn* sculpture entitled "Monument to Work".

Berlin, of course, received special architectural attention. The Olympic Stadium was constructed purposely for the 1936 Olympics, but afterwards became a focal centre for Nazi Party rallies and ceremonies. In March 1934 Troost died, and a new state architect was needed to fill his shoes. Enter Albert Speer, whose style would come to symbolize National Socialist ideology at its

purest. Speer had been a Nazi Party member from 1934. He first demonstrated his talents to Hitler through an innovative use of flagpoles and lighting effects for a massive Nazi rally at Templehof Field on 1 May 1933. When Troost died the following year, Speer's career took off.

Speer became General Architectural Inspector of the Reich in 1937, and was tirelessly employed in redeveloping and designing state architecture. He perfectly understood Hitler's architectural desires. One of Speer's most prestigious early works was the remodelling of the huge Zeppelin Field arena at Nuremberg for Nazi Party rallies. The first temporary reviewing stand featured a massive metallic eagle-and-swastika design, with a wingspan of over 30m (100ft). In 1934 this was replaced by a monolithic structure of marble stairs and colonnades, the facade stretching

Above: The Vienna State Opera House, which Hitler sketched as a youth before World War I and which inspired him to rebuild Berlin in a similar style when he became Führer in January 1933.

97

some 396m (1300ft) in length and rising 24m (80ft) high. When packed with over 300,000 Nazi supporters, ringed with Nazi flags, and lit by celestial shafts of light from military searchlights, the Zeppelin Field Stadium was awesome to behold.

Speer was then given the role of remodelling Berlin itself. By the mid-1930s Hitler envisaged a German Empire – *Germania* – stretching across Europe with Berlin as its centrepiece. Back in 1925, Hitler had already sketched some architectural ideas for a Berlin boasting its conquests. He envisaged a massive triumphal arch elevated to 99m (325ft) – the height intended to dwarf Paris' Arc de Triomphe – inscribed with the names of all Germany's World War I dead. He discussed these ideas with Speer, who then began to plan an epic city redevelopment.

The plans, transferred in exhausting detail into 1/50th scale models by professional cabinet makers, were magisterial. Berlin was to be reconstructed along two north-south and east-west axes. The north-south axis featured a 2.5km- (4-mile-) long boulevard lit by 400 street lights and straddled by Hitler's triumphal arch. The view through the arch led to a Great Hall at the end of the boulevard, capped by a massive dome and offering a 150,000-person capacity. The boulevard would be lined with grand official buildings, and the city as a whole was to be enhanced by numerous non-government developments such as a 2000-seat cinema, a 21-storey hotel, and a public swimming pool constructed in the style of a Roman baths.

The reconstruction of Berlin was never realized. Building began in earnest, but war halted production. It is a testimony to the strength of Hitler's architectural fantasies that there are pictures taken in February 1945 of Hitler assessing models of intended post-war reconstructions (by architect Hermann Giesler) of Linz, his hometown, even as the Russians were battering their way into the capital.

Above: Newly built houses for workers at the I.G. Faben chemical works. Theses dwellings are not typical of the inadequate accommodation for German workers before and during World War II.

Having considered monumental urban development, what was the condition of general housing in Germany during the Nazi years? Whereas Hitler wanted an imperious style for his state architecture, for domestic dwellings he yearned for vernacular German folk styles. In the countryside it was feasible to create, say, the thatched roofing and exposed eaves of traditional housing, but in the city there were much more functional requirements, especially as the urban population grew explosively, even doubling in towns such as Magdeburg and Halle.

Urban housing problems were solved by the production of 300,000 housing units each year, although many of these dwellings were created by splitting up existing properties into smaller apartments. The subsequent standard of urban housing for working-class families was almost invariably poor. One style of flat called the *Volkswohnung* ("People's Flat") was only 36 sq. m (387 sq. ft) for a family of four. The Nazis also produced a high

percentage of medium-sized (three–four bedrooms) dwellings too large, and therefore too expensive, for the vast majority of workers. Chronic overcrowding resulted in many urban districts, as well as impoverished living conditions. A DAF survey in 1937 found that from a 2000-home survey 22 percent had no direct water supply, and 96 percent no bathrooms or showers.

Above: Architecture of the new Germany. The Brown House (party headquarters) in Munich (top), and a model of the huge stadium at Nuremberg (above) being inspected by Hitler and a young Albert Speer, 1933.

Housing development in Germany's towns and cities declined dramatically during the war – only 28,000 new units were built in 1944. Air raids added to the misery, depriving the population of four million apartments and even resulting in bed-share schemes between night and day workers. Hitler's architectural dreams, like so many of his schemes, did not lift the lives of most people.

Hitler had a special philosophical attachment to the countryside. The early Nazi Party was permeated by a *Blut und Boden* (Blood and Soil) movement which rejected urban cosmopolitanism in favour of a nostalgic agriculturalism. In Nazi racial and political theory, the countryside embodied the purest Aryan strains of the German population, without the multicultural "interbreeding" so common in the cities. Land workers were also more in touch with the simple, hard living Hitler eulogized, opposed to the feeble intellectualism present in urban populations.

As Hitler came to power in 1933, agricultural Germany was in deep crisis. The depression of the late 1920s had hit the agrarian communities hardest of all. The collapse in consumer goods prices forced already spartan living conditions well below the poverty line as debt and under-investment crushed many farm businesses. In 1932 agricultural debt stood out at RM10.6 billion, and 15 percent of agricultural income went to paying bank interest.

A range of measures was introduced to restore agricultural prosperity. Crippling debts were rescheduled or set at lower rates, and mortgage rates in general were

Above: The clean lines of a residential building designed by Walter Gropius, a firm believer in standardization and prefabrication. However, few German workers could afford such living quarters.

dropped to around 4.5 percent. Development loans for the purchase of farming technology, storage and labourers' housing became more readily accessible and on more favourable terms. Farmers also benefited from expanding markets. The exodus to urban areas may have purged the countryside of labour, but it also raised the number of city consumers for agricultural produce. Similarly, the massive programmes of conscription into the armed forces produced lucrative contracts supplying food, horses or even land for military use.

The Reich Food Estate

A new organization, the Reich Food Estate, was created to oversee Germany's food production. It was headed by Richard Walter Darré, *Reichsbauernführer* (Reich Agricultural Leader) and *Reichsernnahrungsminister* (Reich Food Minister), himself a former pig farmer. (Darré was also a keen "Blood and Soil" advocate. In 1929 he had published a book entitled *The Peasantry as the Life Source of the Nordic Race*.) The Reich Food Estate was a potent instrument of state, with around three million farms under its jurisdiction. It was meant to provide protection from the market for German farmers while also satisfying Germany's agricultural production needs. Under its jurisdiction fell almost every aspect of a German farm's existence, including crop types, production quotas, technology allocations and, crucially, the prices of goods and wages. Darré's control of the latter elevated the wholesale price of goods by a minimum of 20 percent between 1933 and 1935, vegetables, cattle and dairy produce seeing the steepest rises. But the prices were then passed onto the consumer, and farmers experienced a 34 percent wage increase in the same period. The wage rise was helped by the general

farming exemption from unemployment insurance or health insurance payments.

Other laws were designed to control the sale of agricultural land. In 1933 the Reich Entail Farm Law was introduced to protect farmers against losing their farms through bankruptcy. At the same time Darré brought in the Hereditary Farm Law. Farms of up to 123 hectares (308 acres) in size became hereditary estates which could not be disposed of or divided up to satisfy debt or produce income. Upon the death of the farmer, the land would pass into the ownership of the eldest son alone, who was then under obligation to provide for his relatives. Darré saw this as a way of passing on farming to future generations and so guaranteeing Germany's ambitions of agricultural self-sufficiency in the long term.

Country life

Nazi policies were in many ways beneficial for agriculture – taxes alone were reduced by around 60 percent for most farmers. However, the investment in farming could never conceal the fact that agriculture came second to industry and rearmament in Nazi economics. Food production targets set by the Reich Food Estate began to creep beyond farms' capabilities, forcing them to invest heavily in machinery or fertilizers, driving up their costs. At the same time the fixed prices of goods in the shops made the sale of much produce unprofitable.

The Reich Food Estate became increasingly authoritarian as the years passed. It created dossiers on every single farm in the Third Reich, and closely monitored the progress of everything from quota fulfilment to quality of produce. It produced the most rigorous quota prescriptions – a single hen, for instance, was required to lay 65 eggs a year. The Estate

could also direct a farm to switch its production to a different type of crop, regardless of whether that crop would enhance the profitability of the business.

Debt reappeared – by 1938 it equalled the total value of German farm production. The massive estates of German aristocrats in East Prussia could weather these changes, but small farms could not and lost up to one in three of their workers. The workers that remained had to live on appalling wages. After the fixed costs of maintaining a farm, a farmer's annual income might be only 240 marks, and a farm worker would typically receive around 400 marks less than the wage of a semi-skilled industrial labourer while working nearly double the hours. Government grants and children's allowances aided some farming families, but many workers lived in impoverished conditions.

The state of farm housing was an acute problem. Large estate owners were encouraged to invest in good-

quality housing for workers through the carrot of tax incentives and grants, and the stick of legal action for poor-quality housing provision. Nevertheless the agrarian community remained locked in hardship, with an estimated 300,000 dwellings short of the actual requirement. Over 60 percent of farms did not have piped water. Tractors were relatively scarce compared to Great Britain or the US, meaning that land often had to be ploughed using oxen or horses. Most farm jobs such as bailing were

Above: Scenes from German agriculture in the 1930s. A cattle market in Regen (top) and women farm workers weeding near Tharle. Agriculture was blighted by poor wages, poor housing and long hours.

Left: Ploughing a field in Pomerania, 1935. Despite the availability of tractors, many German farms could not afford to purchase them. As a result, most field work had to be carried out manually.

performed manually, despite technology being available. The combination of poor wages, bad housing, long hours and mounting debt more than explains the exodus of workers to the city. Sensing a labour crisis, in 1934 the Nazi Government passed legislation forcing agricultural labourers to stay in their jobs. The law was rescinded in 1936 as unhappiness reached boiling point and as Nazi urban-based industries demanded surplus German labour.

The problems of farming produced some unexpected social effects. A lack of family housing resulted in very low rates of marriage among farm labourers and rural women. Women also found themselves increasingly responsible for the running of entire farms, as wartime conscription took away large proportions of the menfolk. Even in peacetime women made up a full 50 percent of agricultural workers (75 percent of whom worked unpaid), and could easily put in 70-hour weeks keeping farm and family running. Young single women were a significant element of the rural flight to the city, looking to marry outside the agricultural sector and so improve their prospects and lifestyle. The Nazis arguably helped foster this movement. Women's groups flourished in the Third Reich, some without state approval but many falling under the umbrella of the *National Socialist Frauschaften* (Women's Organization). Agrarian women's groups arranged day trips taking them beyond the confines of

their village to other villages or to towns and cities. Such trips often dispersed young women's parochialism, and gave the women a desire for more than their home region could offer.

Criminality (in the Nazi definition) also rose, expressed usually through involvement in the black market. The main forms of black marketeering in the countryside were the illicit slaughter of livestock or the retention of portions of crops for personal use or private sale. The *schwarschlachten* (black slaughtering) might explain how the livestock populations of cattle, pigs and chickens remained virtually unchanged from 1935 to 1940. Rural areas were far less intensively policed than towns and cities, so afforded greater opportunities for siphoning off food supplies. Yet the dangers of black marketeering were profound. A prison sentence of over one year prohibited future farm ownership, and the illegal slaughter of significant numbers of livestock could and often did receive a death sentence.

Early on in the Nazi regime, Hitler and his officials realized that the drain of agricultural labour had to be reversed. An initial solution was young temporary labourers in the

form of Hitler Youth members, students, schoolchildren and other juvenile workers. Working on the land was deemed edifying to the character, so the Nazi Party had no trouble representing this huge source of school-age free labour as part of a socially valuable "land service" programme. Agricultural apprenticeships were also established in 1937 though proved unpopular, with only one-quarter of the 41,000 positions filled.

Above: Nazi attempts to alleviate the plight of agriculture included drafting in *Reichsarbeitsdienst* (RAD) – National Labour Service – members. These comprised males aged 18–25.

Left: Foreign workers were drafted in large numbers to work in German agriculture. These are young female Eastern European workers (note the "Ost" badge on their clothing). This image is dated 1943.

Foreign adults proved a better remedy to rural labour problems. Italian and Hungarian workers, desperate to escape the economic hardships of their own countries, flocked into Germany to assist with harvesting, 100,000 in 1938 alone. With wartime, the reserve of foreign labour expanded enormously, though this time the labour was forced. Out of a total of 7,126,000 foreign labourers in Germany in 1944, 2,402,000 were sent into agriculture. Polish farm workers had been employed on German farms even before the war, and again Poland was the main source of foreign land labourers.

Foreign workers

The large numbers of foreign labourers in a German agricultural population of only around 13 million gave cause for concern among Nazi civil servants. Most Polish workers were kept housed in camps, and those who lived on smaller farms had to be given separate accommodation on Nazi orders. However, many German farmers became close to the labourers, and the level of segregation often relaxed, particularly on small and isolated farms more resistant to Nazi ideology and observation. Workers from Western European nations such as France and Belgium were almost always treated more leniently, being free from the *untermenschen* category applied to most Eastern Europeans.

A particular danger for women in rural areas was entering into sexual relations with foreign labourers. The risks were increased by the dearth of young men on the land by 1944. Isolated, hard worked and often lonely, women were known to strike up close friendships with the foreigners, friendships which sometimes developed into more. The crime was a serious one in Nazi eyes. Laws against "race defilement" were harsh, and the foreign male would usually be executed (almost always if he was a Pole or Russian). The women would suffer imprisonment. As "imprisonment" could be in a Nazi concentration camp, the sentence could in effect be a death sentence.

War demolished the countryside no less than the towns and cities. Life generally became even harder for rural workers. With so many of Germany's young men away at war, a rural workforce of women or men of advanced age had to work longer hours, often in excess of 100 hours per week during the harvest time. Much worse was to come. In 1945 the Soviet Red Army spilled into Germany itself. Such was the quite legitimate fear of the Russians that almost the entire population of East Prussia, a mainly agricultural region, attempted to flee westwards in the depth of winter, in one of the biggest depopulations in history. It is estimated that nearly one million of them died of exposure, malnutrition, or Red Army vengeance. Such was a cruel end for many who had already endured over a decade of physical hardship working on the land under National Socialist rule.

Above: The Hitler Youth was also used in agriculture. It was considered part of the hardening process. As Hitler stated: "The weak must be chiselled away. I want young men and women who can suffer pain."

Chapter 7
Sport

The Nazis embraced sport enthusiastically, seeing it as an important part of creating an Aryan master race. The result was a physically and mentally tough generation of adults who went on to fight, and die, in the German armed forces in World War II.

The Nazis' enthusiasm for sport is inseparable from their equal passion for war. In 1933 sport fell under the Nazi policy of *Gleichschaltung* – "coordination". *Gleichshaltung* was the attempt to unify the whole of German society and culture behind Nazi doctrine. Even sport was no longer an innocent pursuit. Instead, it became a central pillar of Nazi social engineering. By compelling almost all sectors of German society to engage in regular physical activity, Hitler's regime intended to produce a physically strong and mentally tough nation equipped for its inevitable destiny –

war. As Josef Goebbels, the Reich Minister of Propaganda, readily admitted in a speech on 23 April 1933: "German sport has only one task: to strengthen the character of the German people, imbuing it with the fighting spirit and steadfast camaraderie necessary in the struggle for its existence."

As we shall see, Nazi ideology held physical strength as a supreme virtue, higher than intellectual, even moral, strength. In Hitler's ironic world view, intellectual ability produced feeble-minded individuals unsuited to the great military enterprise Germany was embarking

Below: In Nazi Germany there was a wide range of sports available, from fencing (left) to swimming (right). But all were designed to give Germany's young people "hard and strong" bodies.

upon. This attitude is most clearly seen in Hitler's attitudes towards youth, the main target for the Nazi sporting programme.

Sport and youth

In one of his most famous quotations, the Führer expressed his desire for a youth "quick like greyhounds, tough like leather, and as hard as Krupp steel". To fulfil Hitler's wish, the youth sport system in Nazi Germany was geared up to violently competitive games with pain and exhaustion as standard ingredients. The rationale behind this approach is found in another of Hitler's speeches. Youth, according to Hitler, will be:

fully trained in all physical exercises. I intend to have an athletic youth, that is the first and the chief thing. In this way, I shall eradicate the thousands of years of human domestication. Then I shall have in front of me the pure and noble natural material. With that, I can create a new

order. The whole education in a national state must aim not to stuff the student with mere knowledge, but to build bodies which are healthy to the core. I will have no intellectual training. Knowledge is ruin to my young men. A violently active, dominating, brutal youth – that is what I am after. Youth must be indifferent to pain. There must be no weakness and tenderness in it. I want to see once more in its eyes the gleam of pride and independence of the beast of prey.

Essentially Nazi sport was a method of erasing all vestiges of humanity and tenderness prior to conscription, at which point the resculptured individual would be militarily useful. It is no coincidence that many of the most fanatical youngsters this regime produced served in the SS death squads on the Eastern Front.

In the mid-1930s, all schoolchildren were required to do two or three sessions of physical

Above: As well as keeping bodies healthy, physical activities were designed to deflect young German people away from "harmful activities such as card playing, drinking alcohol and bad music".

training per week. By 1938 the number of sessions had risen to five (at the expense of religious education). Sporting activities were not only practised within school, but also in various Nazi youth organizations attended after school, at the weekends, or during special camps. There were four principal organizations. For boys the *Deutsches Jungvolk* (German Young People) and *Hitlerjugend* (Hitler Youth) handled, respectively, the 10–14 and 14–18 age groups. The same age groups for girls were split between the *Jungmädelbund* (Young Girls League) and the *Bund Deutscher Mädel* (League of German Girls). "Promising" male teenagers might also attend one of the three youth leadership schools: the *Adolf Hitler Schule* (Adolf Hitler School), the *Nationalpolitische Erziehungsanstalten* (National Political Training Institutes, or "Napolas"), or the *Ordensburgen* (Order Castles).

Within these institutions, more time was taken up with physical training than any other activity. The range of sports was extremely broad. Almost every event in athletics and gymnastics was featured, but especially long-distance running, swimming, long jump, discus and hammer throwing. Nazi youth sport programmes also aimed to produce military skills and what could be termed a "unit psychology". Sporting activities in the Hitler Youth were scarcely veiled infantry training programmes. During the 1933–35 period, when the Versailles Treaty banned many forms of war preparation, the category "sports" included shooting, sailing, flying gliders, map reading, transporting gun limbers and erecting camouflage. All this was conducted in military style uniforms and medals were awarded to those individuals who did well in the activities. Once the Versailles Treaty was lifted in 1935 these activities became slightly more transparent, but there was still an attempt to conceal the real purpose under the mask of sport. Only in the late 1930s did Hitler Youth training show its true colours when the content of its training fell under the direct jurisdiction of the *Wehrmacht*. (One benefit of the *Wehrmacht* authority was the banning of boxing matches between boys unless under the direct supervision of officers, although whether this led to less brutalization is debatable.)

The combination of practical military training and sport was meant to inculcate team-working skills among the young. Like most totalitarian regimes, Nazi Germany was radically anti-individual. Games were devised to inculcate a sense of belonging towards the group and the team rather than the self. This is not

as wholesome as it sounds. One game, for example, was called "Trapper and Indian". Two teams distinguished by different coloured armbands would track each other through dense forest using techniques of camouflage, patrol and ambush. One team would attempt to surprise the other, and in little more than a sanctioned scuffle each person attempted to rip off the "enemy" armbands and defeat the opposing team. Although such games were supervised by platoon leaders known as *Scharführeren*, the violence could be substantial. Only those youngsters who were physically well-developed and extremely motivated did well. Poor performers would be eventually ostracized by their team-mates and by camp leaders, and subjected to bullying and menial labour as punishment for physical weakness.

For thousands of less able or nervous children throughout the Third Reich, sport amounted to an instrument of torture. Boxing was a compulsory activity in schools or youth camps for many older boys, an activity consigning many children to a weekly beating at the hands of some pitiless thug. Even less violent games took their toll. Many games were pursued to the point of exhaustion, and rates of physical injury and nervous exhaustion rocketed. Physical damage became an acute problem. The growth plates in human bones are particularly vulnerable to injury if subjected to high stress in teenagers, exactly the demographic group targeted by Nazi Germany's most intensive sports regime. In 1936 around 37 percent of the 18-year-old individuals called up for military service were suffering from flat feet caused by collapsed arches. One youth leader in Hanover had to order an immediate decrease in physical activity to control the problem among his wards.

Psychological and social problems were also created. Many school entrance exams included sport, so those lacking athleticism could struggle to enter education regardless of their intelligence. Furthermore, a school-leaving certificate was issued only to those who attained the recommended sporting standards. Young adults who had just left school and embarked on apprenticeships were obliged to continue the school fitness programme for the duration of

Above: In Nazi Germany sport and military training often merged. Here, for example, a Hitler Youth member prepares for a flight in a flying glider boat. No doubt he later entered Göring's *Luftwaffe*.

Left: "We do not want this nation to become soft. Instead, it should be hard and you will have to harden yourselves while you are young. You must learn to accept deprivations." Hitler addressing the Hitler Youth, 1934.

their apprenticeship. If that wasn't enough, a poor performance in sport at school might lead to suspension, even expulsion. In the warped Nazi view, such failures indicated that the person was worthless in the service of the Third Reich. Little wonder that in a random assessment of a Hitler Youth camp in 1938, 50 children aged between 10 and 15 were diagnosed with chronic stomach disorders related to nervous tension.

For those youths, however, who excelled at sport, the mid- to late-1930s must have been a happy time. Sporting prowess brought recognition from one's peers and leaders, and could place the young person on a fast-track to becoming a military officer. Talent in sport also brought opportunities to compete in national events. In 1935 Baldur von Schirach – the leader of the Hitler Youth – declared "The Year of Physical Training" and also launched the National Sports Competition. This annual competition allowed young people to compete at high standards, and became an enormous event attracting thousands of competitors.

The sporting activities of German youth also benefited the German infrastructure. One of the physical activities of the Hitler Youth was the construction of Youth Hostels. Von Schirach boasted during the Nuremberg trials after World War II that in one year alone his organization had constructed 1000 youth hostels across Germany. Considering that by 1939 nearly nine million young Germans were members of the Hitler Youth, the organisation provided a massive wellspring of free labour for the German regime.

Adults and sport

Youth occupied an unfair amount of sporting attention in the Nazi regime. Yet the adult population did not escape attention, and sporting activities became standard for almost

Below: German girls taking part in an 80m hurdles race. A consequence of the Nazi obsession with sporting prowess was an alarming growth in serious sports injuries among German youths.

all working German citizens between the ages of 16 and 55.

In the Nazi centralized state calisthenics formed part of the working day for most employees in industrial sectors. Entire factories would come to a halt for periods of up to half an hour to perform stretching, strength-building and aerobic exercises. These periods were to contract and often disappear as the Third Reich began its death-slide during World War II. By 1944 even women – traditionally consigned to domesticity in Nazi doctrine – were working in excess of 55 hours a week keeping the German war machine alive. In such a climate additional sporting activities were an intolerable addition.

The price of fitness

Even before the onset of war in 1939, Nazi physical training doctrine was placing a heavy burden on many. One particularly ruthless edict in the late 1930s set physical tests for all German adult males up to the age of 55. The test included a long-jump of 2.8m (9.2ft), a 1km (0.6-mile) run in under six minutes, and hurling a 2.9kg (6.5lb) medicine ball a distance of 6.15m (20ft). For those older participants, such tests frequently resulted in pulled backs, torn ligaments and tendons, and physical exhaustion. Failing the test could mean additional training, and even employment difficulties. The Germany railway system, for example, required a National Sports Certificate as a precondition to employment.

As with youth, sport for Germany's adult population was a mixed blessing. On the one hand, cases of physical injury soared, as did the incidents of nervous illness. From 1933 to 1939 the German suicide rate climbed beyond the average, and overuse of drink and alcohol rose. In some parts of Germany admissions to

mental asylums increased by around 30 percent (although much of the increase may be accounted for by the influx of mentally disabled individuals considered "undesirable" by the regime). Obviously, one must be cautious of ascribing responsibility to sport. Rather, sport was another example of the increasing pressure to perform within German society. Longer working hours, the threat or reality of war and psychological hardship all played their part.

Equally, Nazi sports programmes must have benefited the health of many adults. Over five million Germans, for example, achieved their National Sports Certificates through the *Kraft durch Freude* (KdF; Strength through Joy) movement. There is little direct evidence of how the prevalence of sporting activity among the German population impacted on health. One of the primary benefits of regular exercise is a reduction in incidents of heart disease, strokes and cancer, the three main killers of human beings. Bearing this in mind, the life expectancy of the German population did climb during the peacetime years. In 1910, for example, the life expectancy at birth for a man was 45 years, and for women 48 years. By the late 1930s this ascended to 60 years and 63 years respectively, indicating improvements not only in health care, but also in the general condition of the population.

Above: One of the Nazi regime's Order Castles. The very best pupils went to Order Castles, which were schools that took pupils to the limits of physical endurance. War games used live ammunition.

There were, however, several groups of German people for whom Nazi sport programmes held no benefit whatsoever.

Sport and racial doctrine

The idealized Nazi images of blonde-haired, blue-eyed athletes were not just intended for inspiration. They were, in fact, functioning elements in racial doctrine. Fundamentally, the sporting prowess of German people was meant to demonstrate the physical and mental superiority over non-Aryan peoples, especially Jews and gypsies.

Evidence for this comes in an announcement from the Reich Sport Commissar on 6 August 1935. From this date all German sports clubs had to dedicate the month of October to the teaching of anti-Semitism and Nazi racial doctrine. Crude sessions of pseudo science were the result. Classic Aryan youths were extracted from the clubs' top performers, and used to illustrate perfect Aryan physique and physiognomy. Conversely, pictures of Jewish youths and actual Jewish individuals would be subjected to degrading physiological analysis, teaching the approved athletes "how to spot" a Jew from an Aryan German by looking at key characteristics of face and body structure. Another landmark event of 1935 was a law forbidding Jews from entering military service in the German Army. As sport in Nazi Germany was almost entirely a preparation for military service, it sent a double signal that Jews had no part in Germany's future, either as sportsmen or soldiers.

As sporting activity for most of the German population increased under the Third Reich, therefore, for Jews and other marginalized groups sport declined at both amateur and professional levels. At the amateur level, Jewish athletes and gymnasts were expelled or barred from all school, college, town and regional sports clubs. In defiance many Jews set up their own local clubs, but running these became next to impossible under Nazi persecution. Not only were the athletes targeted for attack, but the clubs received no funding from German education authorities. Attempts at self-funding were gradually eroded as the Nazis steadily barred Jews from employment and commercial activity, even stopping benefit payments then imposing a "compensation fee" on German Jews of RM1000 million in November 1938. Once all Jewish children were excluded from school education in the same month, then Jews had almost no ability to access formal, organized sport at any level.

The policy of excluding Jews and gypsies from sport also impacted on professional games. At the beginning of the 1930s Germany had many sporting champions of Jewish birth. With Hitler's ascent to power, these

Above: The Nazi image of Aryan women. Images such as this were not only intended to show the athleticism of Germans in general; but were also to demonstrate physical superiority over "lesser" races.

athletes became an embarrassment to the Nazi regime – Jews and gypsies were meant to illustrate physical inferiority to Aryan Germans, not athletic prowess. Steadily, therefore, they were purged from competitive sport. In boxing, for example, the Jewish amateur champion Eric Seelig and the gypsy middleweight boxing champion Johann "Rueklie" Trollman were both expelled from the German Boxing Association (Trollman was forbidden to practice boxing at all). In tennis the Jewish international medal winner Daniel Prenn was ejected from the German Davis Cup Team, while the high jumper Gretel Bergmann could not find a club to accept her apart from the Jewish *Der Schild* (The Shield) association.

It was equally perilous for non-Jewish athletes to maintain associations with Jewish sportsmen and women. On 3 July 1935, for example, the official newspaper of the SS, *Das Schwartze Korps (The Black*

Above: Women were expected to be fit, but not too slim, which was believed to cause problems in pregnancy.

Left: Hans von Tschammer und Osten (right), Reich Sport Leader. He made sporting prowess a criterion for entrance to schools and certain jobs.

Corps) – Hitler's bodyguards – wrote that "there was criticism of the fact that in Berlin a group of Jewish women competed with the group of sports women of the police sports clubs of Berlin. We have investigated

113

this fact and are glad to announce that all the members who have participated in this game had been excluded from German sports organizations."

An exception to Jewish exclusion was the half-Jewish fencing champion Helene Mayer. She actually represented Germany in the 1936 Olympics in Berlin, although, as we shall see, she competed only because the German regime needed to create the appearance of liberalism for the

international community. An earlier Nazi decree made clear that 1936 would be a watershed for Jewish athletes. It stated that "to gag the Jewish agitation from abroad ... Jews (without any close contact with non-Jews) ... are allowed to practice [sport] until the Olympics 1936. A general regulation for Jewish sports will come out after the end of the Olympics." The "general regulation" referred to nothing less than the

Above: The US heavyweight boxer Joe Louis (right). In 1937, he defeated world heavyweight champion James J. Braddock. He then stated: "I don't want nobody to call me champ until I beat Max Schmeling."

114

expulsion of Jewish people from the German sporting community.

Another sector of society excluded from sport in Germany was black people. German blacks were categorised as *untermenschen* – sub-humans – along with other races such as Russians and Poles. Yet on the international circuit German athletes faced direct competition from black athletes. In the United States, despite segregation and racism still being widespread, significant numbers of blacks were competing at the highest levels in sport, especially in boxing and running. So when German sportsmen met black Americans in competition, more was at stake than athletic ability.

Max Schmeling and Joe Louis

Such was the case in the epic battle between the German boxer Max Schmeling and his black American rival, Joe Louis. By the mid-1930s Joe Louis was a rising star in international heavyweight boxing. He dealt his first blow against fascism in 1935 when he defeated Primo Carnera, the Italian heavyweight champion, in just six rounds. The US public was confident that Louis would thrash his next opponent, the former German heavyweight champion Max Schmeling. The fight was scheduled for 19 June 1936.

It was a contest heavily infused with ideology. Louis himself had struggled against racism within the US sports community, but through a good promoter was gradually accepted by the white sporting fraternity. The US Jewish population was especially eager to see him smash the German boxer and dent the confidence of German racial superiority. Across the Atlantic, the Germans also realized that much was at stake, as Schmeling was promoted as a specimen of supreme Aryan breeding.

Left: A confident Max Schmeling arrives in the United States for his re-match with Joe Louis in June 1938. Schmeling was projected as the symbol of Nazi Germany and Aryan supremacy.

In the US Schmeling was massively underestimated. He had been heavyweight champion in 1930 and 1932, but now was under betting odds of 10-1 against. Louis himself believed this propaganda, and slackened his training schedule in preference for the golf course. It was a big mistake. On the night of the fight, in front of 45,000 people at the Yankee Stadium, Schmeling battered Louis for round after round until Louis went down and out in the 12th.

The victory caused dismay in the United States, euphoria in Nazi Germany. In the Nazi worldview, Schmeling's triumph confirmed the position of white German manhood over "lesser" races. Schmeling became a national hero. Hitler himself cabled Schmeling directly and praised him for a "splendid patriotic achievement".

It was not the end of the story. In 1937 Louis won the heavyweight championship back after defeating James J. Braddock. A re-match with Schmeling was scheduled. This time, the ideological fervour was even greater as a heavyweight championship was at stake. The match was seen entirely in national

115

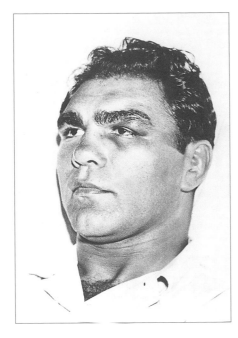

and racial terms. By 22 June 1938, the date of the contest, the US public was intimately acquainted with the facts about German political and racial intolerance. With its massive Jewish and African-American communities, the US lent on Louis to produce victory. President Franklin Roosevelt himself told Louis at a White House dinner: "Joe, we need muscles like yours to beat Germany." Schmeling's arrival by ship at New York harbour was greeted by hundreds of demonstrators from the Anti-Nazi League and the American Jewish Congress. Schmeling himself received another telegram from Hitler: "To the coming World Champion, Max Schmeling. Wishing you every success."

This time, Louis was ready. In front of a 70,000-strong crowd, again in the Yankee Stadium, a 40-punch barrage from Louis finished the fight in the first round in two minutes and four seconds. The result dismayed the German authorities, who quickly distanced themselves from Schmeling. In the United States the *American Hebrew* summed up the

mood by saying that Louis had struck "a terrific blow to the theory of race supremacy". The ironic counter note is that neither of the protagonists were really interested in politics. Schmeling, in fact, was actively opposed to Nazi racial policy. Louis expressed his feelings: "I had nothing personally against Max. But in my mind, I wasn't champion until I beat him. The rest of it – black against white – was somebody else's talk." Following the war Louis and Schmeling even became firm friends.

The 1936 Olympics

The 1936 Olympics in Berlin is probably the most controversial Olympics in the history of the games. Following World War I, Germany was barred from Olympic participation in 1920 and 1924. This did not unduly trouble Hitler – he felt that competing alongside "inferior non-Aryans" would degrade the German people. Bruno Matlitz, a Nazi spokesman, confirmed these sentiments in a letter to German sports clubs, demeaning the Olympics as "infested with Frenchman, Belgians, Pollacks and Jew-Niggers".

In spite of Nazi views, on 13 May 1931 the International Olympic Committee (IOC) awarded Germany the right to host the 1936 Olympics. The Nazis, of course, were not in power at this time and the IOC felt that the award signalled Germany's return to the fold of civilized nations. Controversy arose after 1933, when the Nazis' fascist and anti-Jewish credentials became government policy. Goebbels persuaded Hitler to review his attitude to the games. He insisted that hosting the Olympics would demonstrate Germany's renewed strength to the international community, and provide first-rate propaganda material. The competition would also enable the undoubtedly strong German team to demonstrate Aryan athleticism. Hitler

Left: Schmeling in a hospital bed following his defeat at the hands of Joe Louis. Schmeling was a paratrooper in World War II and resumed his career when the war ended. He fought until 1948 before retiring.

Opposite: Louis in training for the re-match with Schmeling. This time he took the bout seriously, and trained hard. In the ring Schmeling fell to the floor in just two minutes and four seconds.

117

agreed, and RM20 million ($8 million US) were channelled into the games.

By 1934, however, a major international argument broke out over the German venue. This argument was especially vitriolic in United States. Jewish, Catholic, Christian and secular athletic organizations flocked to denounce the German games. In the words of the IOC president Avery Brundage in 1933: "The very foundation of the modern Olympic revival will be undermined if individual countries are allowed to restrict participation by reason of class, creed, or race." Olympic rules specifically forbade racial or religious discrimination, and many athletes and athletic bodies recommended a complete boycott.

Avery Brundage was actually very much opposed to the boycott, arguing that the Olympic games "belong to the athletes and not the politicians". His motivations became slightly more suspect in 1935 when he alleged that a "Jewish-communist conspiracy" was the real force behind the opposition to the games. This was entirely incorrect, as even some US Jewish athletic organizations opposed the boycott. Yet to deal with

the rising furore, Brundage and IOC officials visited Berlin in 1934 to assess the charges of discrimination. Their visit was carefully stage-managed by the Germans. All evidence of anti-Semitism was removed from the city and the officials were introduced to Jewish athletes who claimed complete freedom in their sport.

Below: The 1936 Winter Olympics was a chance to show off Nazism to the world (bottom). The games attracted the world's top athletes, such as the ice-skater Sonja Henie from Norway (below).

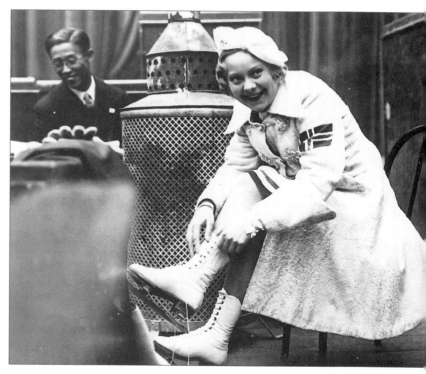

Olympia 1936

The boycott debate was resolved on 8 December 1935 when the Amateur Athletic Union voted to attend the games. Numbers of individual athletes still decided to stay away. An alternative "People's Olympiad" was planned for July 1936 in Barcelona, Spain, but was prevented by the outbreak of the Spanish Civil War.

The games begin

Prior to the Berlin games, Germany also hosted the Winter Olympics at Germisch-Partenkirchen in the Bavarian Alps between 6 and 16 February 1936. The Winter Olympics gave Germany the chance to practice something it would perfect in the Berlin Olympics – the temporary suspension of anti-Semitism for the appearance of international visitors.

Visitors to Berlin in 1936 would be forgiven for thinking that German anti-Semitism was a myth. All anti-Jewish posters and literature were removed. German newspapers were forbidden to print anti-Semitic stories or features during the period of the games. The residents of Berlin were even instructed not to talk about anti-Semitism between 30 June and 1 September. To create the impression that Germany was a liberal nation, the half-Jewish (though very "Aryan" looking) fencing champion Helene Mayer was allowed to compete on the German team. (During the Winter Olympics the half-Jewish ice-hockey player Rudi Ball was also a team member).

Berlin citizens laid on lavish hospitality for visiting athletes and spectators. Egg consumption among Berliners was cut back to allow unfettered consumption by visitors. Anti-homosexual laws were relaxed. The whole city was lavishly bedecked in swastikas and Nazi paraphernalia to give it an energetic and majestic appearance. Military mobilization was

also hidden. Note this instruction from the propaganda office concerning the Olympic village: "The northern section of the Olympic village, originally utilized by the *Wehrmacht*, should not be referred to as *Kasernel* [the barracks], but will hereafter be called 'North Section Olympic Village'." The world's press were almost entirely swayed. Only one or two sage reporters saw behind the façade, and even they didn't see the full truth – in the northern suburbs of Berlin the infamous Oranienburg concentration camp was already filling up with Jews and other persecuted peoples.

The games' opening ceremony was remembered by all who attended. Cannons were fired around the city. Hitler himself released 20,000 carrier pigeons from the *Sportpalast* stadium. The *Hindenburg* zeppelin airship, nearly 304m (1000ft) long, circled over the stadium towing a huge Olympic flag. In the midst of the pomp and ceremony, athletes from 49 nations paraded before the crowds.

Left: At the Winter Olympics Germany came second among the medal-winning countries, taking home three golds and three silvers. Finland, with its seven gold, five silver and three bronze medals, came first.

Ideological defeat

The results of the XI Olympiad in Berlin were generally positive for its German hosts. The enormous investment in athletic training made before the games paid off in 33 gold medals for the German team; other teams were left far behind. For the Nazis, Aryan notions of racehood were validated.

Yet just as many German prejudices were confirmed, some were challenged. The half-Jewish fencer Helene Mayer came third, while Jews from other countries won the gold and silver medals. In a militaristic sport like fencing, the domination by Jewish athletes was a major embarrassment for the Nazis. The embarrassment, however, was qualified by Mayer's sterling additions to Nazi propaganda. She gave the full Nazi salute from the medals podium, and shook hands with Hitler at an Olympic reception. She also

Left: Berlin, 1936. Garlands and shields bearing the coats-of-arms of the nations competing in the games. Hotels were ordered to show extreme tolerance to all visiting foreigners, regardless of race or religious affiliation.

Below: The Brandenburg Gate in Berlin during the 1936 Olympic Games. All anti-Semitic posters had been removed before the games began, and even newspaper vending machines were removed.

participated in the film *Olympia*, a documentary about the games made by the leading film-maker of the Nazi era, Leni Reifenstahl.

A more serious challenge to Nazi dogma came from the US team in the form of the black athlete Jesse Owens. In total the US team won 56 medals during the Berlin Olympics, 14 taken by African Americans. Owens gave an incredible performance. He not only helped the US relay team to gold in the 4 x 100m relay, but also won gold in the 100m sprint, 200m sprint and the long jump.

Jesse Owens' amazing run of victories was genuinely awkward for the Nazis. Goebbels had given instructions to the racist German press not to taunt black athletes during the Olympics. Instead, Owens' achievements were sidelined and Hitler refused to shake hands with Owens or any black athlete. In

the US, meanwhile, Owens' achievements were held up as a defeat for Nazi ideology. The US had some awkward soul-searching to perform, however, in regard to its own race record. An unpleasant incident occurred during the Olympics when Avery Brundage removed Marty Glickman and San Stoller from the US track-and-field relay team. They were the only Jewish men on the team and the action was seen as Brundage's attempt to appease Hitler.

Apart from the achievements of Mayer and black African-Americans, the 1936 Berlin Olympics were undoubtedly a huge success for the Germans. Hitler was so impressed that he told his architectural inspector, Albert Speer, that "in 1940 the Olympic games will take place in Tokyo. But thereafter they will take place in Germany for time to come, in this stadium."

Above: The vast Berlin Olympic stadium held 110,000 spectators. Over 4000 athletes from 49 countries took part in the games. All parades, as shown above, were expertly choreographed.

With the end of the 1936 games the Nazi regime resumed its programme of persecution. Jews faced renewed violence and discrimination within two weeks of the games ending. (Mayer became a US citizen in 1940, changing her surname to Meyer. Her uncle was sent to a concentration camp and murdered.) Germany garnered international respect from the event, sadly. As the circumspect US journalist William Shirer observed on 16 August 1936: "I'm afraid the Nazis have succeeded in their propaganda. First, the Nazis have run the games on a lavish scale never before experienced, and this has appealed to the athletes. Second, the Nazis have put up a very good front for the general visitors, especially the big businessman." Only with the onset of war in 1939 did the world see Germany's true colours.

Above: The US athlete Jesse Owens wins the 200m heat. Hitler refused to meet any black medal winners.

Left: The half-Jewish German fencing champion Helene Mayer. She won a silver medal at the 1936 Olympics.

In April 1945 Soviet forces smashed into Berlin, bringing the war to an end by early May. The infamous *Sportpalast* lay in ruins, smashed by Allied bombing raids and

Soviet artillery fire. Its transformation from a bombastic monolith of German ideology to gutted shell was absolute.

What had sport contributed to the rise and fall of the Nazis? The Nazis undoubtedly created a physically and mentally tough generation of young adults ripe for military service. Post-war analysis showed that in actions where German troops faced Allied soldiers with similar combat strengths on both sides, the Allies usually suffered 50 percent more casualties than the Germans. The excellent quality of German soldiery was as much to do with rigorous *Wehrmacht* training as sport, but there is little doubt that the excellent physical fitness of German soldiers and their familiarity with pressurized competitive environments and military style training helped them to excel on the battlefield.

However, throughout the war certain Allied units showed equal aplomb and grit in combat without the sporting background. Probably the most significant contribution of sport to the Third Reich was its use in racial doctrine. Robert Ley, the leader of the German Labour Front between 1933 and 1945, once expressed his preference for teaching riding to young Nazi leaders. His view was that "there must be great attention paid to riding because it gives ... the feeling of being able to dominate a living creature entirely." This is arguably the subtext of all sporting endeavour during the Nazi period. Sports were used to produce individuals dismissive of human weakness and contemptuous of entire races. As such, the period 1933 to 1945 must contain history's most shameful application of physical development.

Above: Hitler (front row, with swastika armband) at the swimming finals of the 1936 games. Despite the success of black athletes, the Nazis overall were very pleased with the games, as Germany won most medals.

123

Chapter 8
Employment

The Nazis achieved something of an economic miracle in Germany during the 1930s, almost eradicating unemployment and boosting industrial output. However, this was achieved by abolishing trade unions, capping wages and increasing work hours.

Adolf Hitler once said: "Whoever wants to be a true Socialist must first have experienced misery physically, in his own body." This bleak philosophy encapsulates a truth about labour conditions in the Third Reich between 1933 and 1945. Work under the Nazi regime was primarily a form of national service rather than personal vocation. Robert Ley, head of the *Deutsche Arbeitsfront* (DAF; German Labour Front), explained in a 1936 propaganda publication that:

Adolf Hitler created National Socialism, and placed the common good above individual good. The class struggle, whether from above or below, from the right or the left, was raised by him with the proclamation of the honour of work and of service in the people themselves. So that this lesson that made the German Worker the supporter of the State is never lost, the National Socialist Work Service is careful to see that every man who before worked for his own profit now

Below: Unemployed Berliners wait in front of a municipal payment office in late 1930, during the worldwide economic depression that followed the New York stock market crash of October 1929.

must use his creative hands for the profit of the people.

Ley presents labour not as the individual act of earning a living, but as a "service" to the greater good of the German Reich. As in Marxism (though Ley is keen to distinguish his views from those of Marx), individuals have less value than the mass. As we look deeper into the employment system of Nazi Germany, we see that being a worker in the Third Reich was a double-edged sword. On one hand, welcome conditions of near full employment were achieved as work took centre stage in German economics. By contrast, the emphasis that all labour must be directed towards the profit of the state meant that workers' rights and lives were entirely subordinated to Nazi control.

The Nazi economy

In January 1933 unemployment figures in Germany stood at a crippling six million. By January 1939, that figure had fallen to an incredible 302,000. There are some cautions about interpreting the bare statistics, but the undeniable fact is

that Hitler's domestic policies brought conditions of nearly full employment after only six years of Nazi administration. How Hitler achieved this revolution in German labour conditions is intricately bound up with German economic policy.

In early 1933 Germany was still stagnating under the effects of the worldwide economic depression precipitated by the 1929 stock-market crash. Its economic problems appeared insurmountable. There were six million unemployed, with millions more trapped in poverty,

Above: The depression of the early 1930s affected the whole of Weimar Germany. The top picture shows unemployed in Berlin, the one above a dole queue in Hanover in 1933. Note the bicycles.

especially in the agricultural community. A crisis in banking had made investors reluctant to commit venture finance to any project. Germany was trapped in a chronic balance-of-trade deficit: it was importing far more than it exported. Germany had to export more to increase domestic prosperity, but increased prosperity often results in increased imports of foreign goods. If imports dominated exports, then ultimately Germany would struggle to find the financial means to pay for essential imported goods such as food, certain metals and oil.

Dr Hjalmar Schacht

As Hitler took power in 1933, he realized that all his ambitions hinged on restoring economic stability. Yet Hitler, contrary to popular belief, had little ability or interest in economics. So the first man to tackle the tottering German economy was Dr Hjalmar Schacht. Schacht had an excellent financial pedigree. He worked as a financial consultant administrating the German occupation of Belgium in World War I, and in 1916 became director of the German National Bank. By 1923 he was the Reich Currency Commissioner and showed such ability to control Germany's inflation that he subsequently became president of the *Reichsbank* in March 1933, a personal appointment from Hitler.

Schacht also developed prudent political credentials. He became a convert to National Socialism after reading Hitler's *Mein Kampf* in 1930, and by 1931 was working as a Nazi fundraiser. He was also a vehement anti-Semite. In August 1934 Schacht took the lead role in the German economy as the Reich Minister of Economics.

Most experts now agree that the worldwide economy was picking up by 1933 anyway, so the rejuvenation of the German economy is not entirely down to the vision of Hitler or the talent of Schacht. However, the bold economics of the early Nazi regime certainly accelerated the improvement.

Schacht and Hitler developed several key policies for economic turnaround. First was Hitler's personal baby, the concept of "autarky", literally meaning "self-sufficiency". Hitler was always troubled by Germany's dependence on imports, as an ingredient in Germany's defeat in World War I was the blockade of incoming goods by the Allied navies. Autarky meant that all essential products and services – particularly rubber, oil, iron ore, coke and coal – would be sourced within Germany itself or within a German-dominated empire.

Upon autarky hung the next element of economic revival: rearmament. From the outset of his tenure as Chancellor, Hitler desired the creation of a *Wehrwirtschaft*, a defence economy. Germany industry would be massively reconfigured to

Above: Dr Hjalmar Schacht, Reich Minister of Economics. At the Nuremberg trials after World War II he was acquitted of war crimes and later became adviser to Colonel Nasser of Egypt in the 1950s.

make, in Hitler's words, "Germany ready for war again". Accompanying both *Wehrwirtschaft* and autarky was the longer-term ambition of *Lebensraum* ("living space"). Germany simply did not have the geological or agricultural resources to attain total self-sufficiency. Thus Hitler looked to territorial acquisitions to make up the deficit. Conquering the "bread basket" of the Ukraine, for example, would bring Germany the crop-growing resources of that fertile country, while taking the Caucasus offered access to huge oil reserves. The expression of these ambitions was a long way off in 1933, but *Lebensraum* formed the catalyst for Germany's major rearmament programme.

Perhaps the most important element to Schacht's economic policy was the stabilizing of the German domestic economy through reduced unemployment. To kick-start the economy Schacht set in place a range of prudent measures:

Left: Robert Ley (right), head of the German Labour Front who started the Strength through Joy movement. Violently anti-Semitic and a drunkard, he committed suicide at Nuremberg in 1945.

Below: When Hitler came to power he was determined to gear German industry up for war. This meant large-scale rearmament, which greatly benefited weapons manufacturers such as Krupp.

he fixed low interest rates to improve investor confidence, he boosted the finances of local authorities by rescheduling their debts, and share trading was revitalized by the large-scale government repurchase of private shares.

Yet more significant than all these actions, and crucial to understanding the revival of German employment, was Germany's huge programme of public works. Schacht practised the principle of deficit spending – pushing huge volumes of debt-funded government money into schemes to create employment and stimulate the economy. Public investment tripled and government expenditure went up by 70 percent between 1933 and 1936. The money was poured into public building projects and housing development, reforestation, road building, and re-investment in the armed services.

The effect of these policies on German employment was transformatory. The motorway building scheme alone in its first year created around 84,000 jobs, and by the end of 1934 some 1.7 million workers were engaged in public works schemes. The schemes often dovetailed with the rearmament programme. For much of the 1930s

the conditions of the Versailles Treaty prohibited Germany from significant rearmament. Therefore, the construction of runways, barracks and militarily essential features such as roads and railways were placed under the work-creation remit to mask their real purpose. Road-building, for example, fell under the jurisdiction of the Minister of Armaments, Fritz Todt.

Göring takes over

Schacht's early economic policies were vigorously successful, and Germany began to feel a renewed confidence. Unemployment figures during Schacht's period in office between 1933 and 1936 were as follows:

January 1933	6 million
January 1934	3.3 million
January 1935	2.9 million
January 1936	2.5 million

While unemployment plummeted, autarky also made progress. Agricultural output of arable crops and livestock was little changed or had actually dropped from 1935 levels, but by 1936 mineral extraction and iron, steel and chemicals production had nearly doubled from

Below: A German metalworks churns out barrels for naval guns in the late 1930s. Nazi rearmament resulted in a rise in the industrial workforce and a dramatic drop in the number of unemployed.

1933 levels. Against these positive signs was the question of whether Germany could afford its lavish public works and rearmament programmes in the long-term. Seventy percent of the total German state finances were sunk into regeneration projects between 1933 and 1936. Rearmament expenditure alone in 1933 was 2772 million Reichmarks or 6.3 percent of net domestic product, but by 1936 this had risen to 12,325 million Reichmarks, a prodigious 19.4 percent of net domestic product.

Schacht was increasingly unhappy. Autarky was proving extremely expensive, and was of questionable viability. Germany was producing more of its own materials through cheap synthetic substitutes, but even by 1939 a massive 33 percent of essential materials was still being imported. In early 1936 Schacht voiced his concerns. He warned that deficit spending and a mounting balance-of-payments problem were driving Germany deeply into the red. The solution was, Schacht continued, to cut back on the rearmament programme,

re-invest more in supplying consumer goods (particularly food fats, hence the economic argument was known as the "guns or butter" debate), and also increase trade links with foreign countries.

These policy suggestions angered Hitler. Schacht had always found autarky and the war economy questionable, so switched to more conventional financial strategies. In August 1936 Hitler released a memorandum reaffirming his key economic goals. It was clear that Schacht would have to go. In October Schacht was effectively sidelined by the appointment of Hermann Göring as Plenipotentiary of the "Four-Year Plan". The Four-Year Plan replaced Schacht's "New Plan", and was to be the official Nazi economic doctrine from 1936 to 1940. Göring, despite having no economic acumen, oversaw the reaffirmation of autarky, deficit spending and *Wehrwirtschaft* as Nazi policy.

These three cornerstone policies were pursued with renewed vigour under Göring, and Schacht resigned in 1937 in protest. Göring became Minister of the Economy. The trend

Above: A new *Autobahn* in 1937 (left). The *Autobahn* scheme gave a major boost to German employment. Autarky was another Nazi economic aim. But, despite developing synthetic substitutes, Germany still had to import essential, such as oil from Romanian oilfields (right).

129

of reducing unemployment, however, continued unabated. The unemployment figures for 1936 to 1939 were:

January 1936	2.5 million
January 1937	1.8 million
January 1938	1.0 million
January 1939	302,000

The continuing drop in unemployment arose from the increasing demands placed on German productivity. Rearmament and autarky had achieved incredible feats. By 1939 industrial production had increased by around 60 percent from 1933 levels. A total of 3000km (1860 miles) of *Autobahn* had been laid by 1938. In 1936, Germany produced 96,456 tonnes (98,000 tons) of aluminium, but 255,900 tonnes (260,000 tons) in 1942. Mineral oil production leapt from 1,761,800 tonnes (1,790,000 tons) in 1936 to 6,151,570 tonnes (6,250,000 tons) in 1942, and iron ore from 2,219,490 tonnes (2,255,000 tons) to 4,071,850 tonnes (4,137,000 tons) in the same years.

Yet as Schacht had suspected, autarky was still not viable. The Third Reich's own target figures for the materials listed above were 268,700 tonnes (273,000 tons) for aluminium, 13,612,200 tonnes (13,830,000 tons) for mineral oil, 5,461,610 tonnes (5,549,000 tons) for iron ore. In almost every case – except certain useful products like explosives – Germany fell short of reaching its targets. Factor in the massive contribution made by conquered territories after 1939 and we see that autarky remained an elusive goal. Göring was also doing a good job of mismanaging the economy. He controlled vast swathes of German industry and mining, and ultimately had authority over

Below: The synthetic oil plant at Leuna. On 14 December 1933, on behalf of I.G. Farben, Bosch and Schmitz signed a contract with the Nazis to massively expand synthetic oil production at Leuna.

production of coal, iron ore, oil, steel, heavy machinery and armaments. Because of the emphasis on deficit financing, most of these industries were running at a loss. A terrifying illustration of this is that between 1933 and 1939 German state revenue was 62 billion marks, but German state expenditure totalled 101.5 billion marks.

So as Germany moved into war in 1939, we have a split perspective on its economy. On the one hand, the German people were experiencing a time of great financial stability and full employment. On the other hand, the dramatic imbalance of the German economy suggested this prosperity could not last. Many historians feel that Hitler was compelled to go to war in 1939 because of Germany's unsustainable economy – conquest was the only way to address the balance-of-payments deficit.

Our overview of the German economy from 1933 to the outbreak of war is essential for appreciating the condition of workers in the Third Reich. What we see is a German economy desperate to maintain high levels of productivity, keep wages low and control the allocation of labour. Hitler's regime would provide full employment, but at a serious price.

The Deutsche Arbeitsfront (DAF)

In the Third Reich every aspect of labour – wages, mobility, industrial disputes, hours, productivity, perks and benefits – was centrally controlled by the Nazi state. Prior to 1933, the workers were able to represent themselves through trade unions. With the Nazis' abolishment of these organizations, Germany's 20.8-million strong workforce now fell under the "representation" of a new body, the *Deutsche Arbeitsfront* (DAF).

The DAF was part of Hitler's ostensible attempt to bring order and harmony into the German labour community. Dr Robert Ley – an ambitious Nazi politician – first quashed all of Germany's 169 trade unions before heading the DAF when it was formed on 10 May 1933. The apparent purpose of the DAF was to create a cohesive German labour force united behind a powerful, resurgent Germany. It was classless in composition – there was no distinction between white- and blue-collar labourers – and it appropriated all roles previously held by trade unions. The DAF was more concerned with imposing Nazi economic and social policy on the workers. It made sure wages were kept within government limits, and also paid for training and apprenticeships in industries vital to Hitler's reconstruction programme.

Yet the DAF did bring benefits to workers. Two subsections of the DAF were the *Kraft durch Freude* (KdF; Strength through Joy) and the *Schönheit der Arbeit* (SdA; Beauty of Labour) movements. Both were schemes to provide workers with subsidized holidays and other forms of entertainment. The KdF was by far the largest, with 56 million marks

Above: Hermann Göring, head of the *Luftwaffe* and Plenipotentiary of the Four-Year Plan. He famously remarked in 1936: "Would you rather have butter or guns? Should we import lard or metal ores?"

of investment behind it in 1933–36 alone. KdF activities included foreign cruises – the KdF built and owned two luxury cruise liners – foreign holidays (usually by rail) to destinations such as Italy, Portugal and Norway, hiking, sporting pursuits and competitions, dancing, art classes, theatre going and political education classes.

The KdF subsidies were sufficient to see a full 50 percent of German workers go on national holidays in 1938, including 180,000 on foreign cruises. At one end of the scale a week in the Harz Mountains would cost around 28 marks, whereas two weeks in Italy was 155 marks. These figures included the cost of travel, meals and accommodation. The SdA organization also offered a similar, though less extensive, travel service, but in addition strove to improve labour conditions in factories, mines and other workplaces. Access to Nazi holiday services was further enhanced by a general doubling of holiday allowance when compared with workers under the Weimar Republic.

The average worker in 1934 could expect an annual holiday allowance of up to 15 days.

DAF holiday schemes undoubtedly provided the German populace with a quick route to travel and recreation. But there were downsides. Wage levels and working hours, as we shall see, remained harsh during the Third Reich, and the KdF holidays were a way of managing working-class discontent. KdF holidays were also ridden with Nazi indoctrination, intermingled with ideological or racial lectures and Aryan-themed sporting events.

Yet outside of the DAF contribution, many workers felt themselves fairly detached from Nazi politics during the early years of the Third Reich, simply grateful to be in employment. Ernst Bromberg, a fitter for the Krupp steelworks, talks of the separation of work and politics:

No time for it [political activity], when you're on three-shift working. Yes, well obviously if you were on piece work, you didn't have time to make speeches, you

Above: Young children on a Strength through Joy leisure break. Strength through Joy was hugely popular, and through it ordinary Germans saw more of their own country than ever before.

got up in the morning when you had to, you didn't overstretch your break periods – because after all, the money was tempting. I didn't worry any more about the Nazis, put it that way, apart from my Labour Front contribution. I just didn't have anything to do with the Nazis.

Much Nazi influence operated in the background of workers' lives, often without their being aware of it. The DAF was for many the most visible presence of the Nazi regime.

Many DAF schemes served to line the pockets of the Nazi regime. Simply being a member of the DAF required a regular financial contribution, the government receiving billions of marks in extra revenue. Even worse was the KdF purchasing programme for the *Volkswagen* (People's Car). The *Volkswagen* was developed as an all-purpose civilian vehicle, and hailed as a future miracle in popular transportation. Thousands of DAF workers committed themselves to a state vehicle-purchase scheme: five marks per week until the vehicle was

paid for, at which point it would be delivered. The *Volkswagen* programme denuded many German workers of up to one-quarter of their weekly wages, but in 1939 all *Volkswagen* production was turned over to military use and not one civilian received his or her vehicle. Needless to say, no money was returned.

One final important aspect of the DAF was its role in workplace politics. Once the DAF had taken over from the trade unions, it abolished strikes, protests and wage bargaining, slashing worker power (Hitler feared the working class as a potential cauldron of revolution, so was keen to curb its vitality). In the place of trade unions the DAF introduced a new relation into companies. Employers were re-labelled "plant leaders" and employees became "plant followers".

The two groups were meant to maintain harmony through a concept of "social harmony" – Nazi-speak for placing national benefit before individual needs. As Richard Grunberger points out in *A Social*

Below: Building aircraft at the Junkers factory in 1939. All German industrial workers were under the control of the DAF, which abolished strikes and wage bargaining, and workers' rights.

History of the Third Reich, the plant followers had little power over the plant leaders. The plant followers could represent their views through a Council of Trust, a group which oversaw the safety and welfare of workers and operated in a role similar to union shop stewards. Yet if the Council of Trust wished to issue a complaint about the plant leader's behaviour or policy, they had to submit it to the Public Trustees of Labour for a ruling. The Public Trustees of Labour were 13 individuals (one individual for each of Germany's 13 economic regions) appointed by central government to act as arbiters in industrial disputes between workers and employers, and to conclude work contracts. Being in the paid employee of the Nazi government meant that the Trustees of Labour generally supported nothing which disrupted industrial production, and large companies in particular were almost exempt from interference. If the trustees judged that a complaint was without foundation, legal action could be taken against the complainants – a strong disincentive to rocking the boat. Furthermore, plant leaders later gained the power to give, or withhold, exemptions from military service. Once war broke out in 1939, and with the spectre of the Russian Front hanging over every German male from 1941, workers had little impetus to bring complaints against their employers.

The economic agenda of the Third Reich required a strict control over labour allocation. Millions of workers were stripped from consumer

Below: Workers were just small cogs in a large machine. Here, Berlin workers toughen their bodies during an outside exercise session – all part of making workers more efficient.

industries – particularly textile manufacture and food production – and redirected into industrial projects such as rearmament or road building. Some 120,000 workers, for example, were put to work on the new *Autobahn*. In 1938 a Reich "industrial conscription" law enabled the state to recruit people into specific, essential industries. Consequently by 1939 one in every five German workers was employed in heavy industry.

What of the rest? For all Hitler's anti-intellectualism, white-collar employment – particularly within the civil service – grew massively under Nazism. The white-collar workforce increased by 25 percent between 1928 and 1939; the blue-collar workforce by only 10 percent. The Nazi machine produced a huge bureaucracy, especially in the administration of its public works and rearmament, and Nazi Party members flooded into the positions in an attempt to climb the political hierarchy. On average, in 1936 white-collar workers earned more than 50 percent more than blue-collar workers, though some wage disparities were levelled out as the era progressed.

Regardless of the sector of employment, however, Nazi policies kept a strict control over the employment of all the Reich's workers. There were two central methods of control: wages and the *Arbeitsbuch* employment document.

Hitler's economic policies may have created full employment, but that is not the same as prosperity. Schacht and then Göring enforced tough wage restraints to control public spending and inflation. The government attempted to freeze wage levels at 1929 Depression levels. At first this was only partially successful. The sudden demand for skilled labourers in metal, engineering, building and chemical industries resulted in skills shortages, and consequently wage increases of around 30 percent for individuals in those professions. For those in the low-priority consumer industries, wages rises were more in the region of two or three percent.

Hitler's economists remedied the problem of variable wages from around 1937, fixing maximum wage levels and limiting employer subsidies of minor perks such as canteen meals and children's allowances. These measures restricted much labour movement, as there was little financial reason to shift jobs. Poverty also became widespread throughout Nazi Germany. Grunberger points out that in 1937 "under conditions

Above: Three examples of the *Volkswagen* (People's Car). Despite 330,000 workers subscribing millions of marks to the KdF purchasing scheme for the *Volkswagen*, not one vehicle was delivered to the German people.

almost approaching full employment over 10 million people – 16 percent of the population – were still receiving Winter Relief parcels or subsidies."

A large part of the problem was that as wages stuck at 1929 levels the deductions from salaries increased. Apart from regular income taxes, workers had to find the money for DAF contributions, unemployment insurance, health insurance and purchase schemes (such as the People's Car). A 1934 report for the Chancellor's office concluded that out of a typical wage 54 percent would go on food, 30 percent on rent and utilities and 11 percent in payroll taxes and contributions (some sources suggest that these last contributions could be as high as 18 percent of income). For many the only remedy was to take advantage of overtime or piece-rate opportunities. Such options, as we shall see, resulted in cruel working hours.

Poverty is in itself a control on labour, as it restricts opportunities for further employment. But a more direct tool of Nazi labour control was the *Arbeitsbuch*. The *Arbeitsbuch* was an employment document rather like a passport. Introduced between 1935 and 1939, it included a worker's personal information such as date and place of birth, type of employment, previous types and places of employment, job changes within a company, marital status and number of children. This information was duplicated in the local labour office's *Arbeitsbuchkartei* (labour pass catalogue).

The *Arbeitsbuch* had a powerful relationship to labour control. An employee had to hand in the *Arbeitsbuch* at the beginning of employment, and it was held by the employer until the employee's contract finished. As the *Arbeitsbuch* was a pre-requisite of employment, this meant that the employer could prevent the employee from shifting jobs. In key industries such as metalworking and armaments, employers were ordered to retain the *Arbeitsbuch* if the worker quit, preventing him or her taking employment elsewhere and allowing the Nazi regime to control labour allocation. Another effect of the *Arbeitsbuch* was that it gave Nazi authorities complete records of their entire workforce, and could formulate policy or re-allocate workers on the basis of the information.

Working conditions

Labour control can be reasonably benign as long as working conditions are good. For millions of workers in the Third Reich this was far from the case. Long hours became the norm for all German workers as the years went on. In 1933 a typical working week for textile employees was around 36 hours. In the more critical building, mining or engineering industries 60 hours was usual. However, by 1939 all workers were putting in an average of 49 hours a week. For many workers on poor wages essential overtime pushed this figure up dramatically, to nearing 70 hours. Moreover, production quotas enforced on companies meant that the pressures under which employees worked kept pace with the hours.

The combination of poor wages, high stress and long hours resulted in a rocketing industrial accident and illness rate. In 1933 the number of industrial accidents and illnesses stood at 929,000. In 1939 the figure had climbed to 2,253,000. Even allowing for the massive increase in the workforce, the figure still represents a more than 100 percent increase in industrial casualties. Workers on the *Autobahn* fared particularly badly. On average one worker was killed for every 6.4km (4 miles) of motorway laid. These conditions were not even alleviated by good pay and housing – pay would be stopped when bad weather prevented work and workers usually lived in huts by the side of the road.

Interestingly, however, the actual duration of time that Germany's injured or ill workers spent off work declined during the same period. German employers used rehabilitation programmes to get the injured back to work quickly, temporarily placing the employees in lighter work or jobs which did not require use of the injured part of the body. Despite such measures, in many industries productivity per worker actually fell during the early years of the Reich as worker morale deteriorated. Mining output fell by around 12 percent from 1936 to 1938, and building output plummeted by nearly 20 percent in 1938 alone.

Gradually productivity issues were addressed through improvements in working practices, but the biggest transformation of productivity and employment came with war.

Below: The influx of foreign workers as a result of war conquests certainly aided German industry, but did little for the slave labourers. These exhausted Russians are taking a quick break between shifts.

The onset of war in 1939 had a profound impact on employment and labour conditions in Germany. Firstly, millions of young German men were conscripted into the armed forces (4.52 million men by 1939), leaving a huge black hole in the German workforce. The hole was filled in several ways. Existing workers were made to work even longer hours. In 1944 the average working week for men was around 70 hours; for women, 54 hours. These figures should be read against the drop in German food rations throughout the war. In September 1939, an adult would receive a limitless ration of bread, 0.55kg (1.2lb) of meat, and 0.31kg (0.68lb) of fat products per week. In March 1944 the ration was around 2.5kg (5.5lb) of bread, 0.36kg (0.7lb) of meat and 0.22kg (0.44lb) of fat. Although the rations were above subsistence level, working such hideous hours on a restrictive diet must have been shattering for

individuals. Many factories began supplementing workers' energy levels with vitamin pills and calisthenics in the workplace.

Women workers

Women made the biggest contribution to wartime labour. In 1939 women constituted 37.4 percent of the total German workforce. By 1944, the figure stood at 50.7 percent, a total of 14.5 million female workers. After women, the Third Reich also solved its labour problems by purging the occupied territories of vast amounts of forced labour. In 1939 301,000 foreign civilians were transported to the Reich, but by 1944 there were 5,295,000 plus 1,831,000 POW labourers. In that year foreign workers made up 24 percent of the entire German workforce, and around 20,000 work camps were built to house the foreign labour. Poland alone produced nearly 1.5 million labourers for the Reich. Around 80 percent of them worked in

Opposite: The outbreak of war in 1939 meant the German economy lost millions of men to the armed forces. To fill this vacuum women were drafted into industry. Here, female workers make army uniforms.

Below: Part of the massive Krupp steel works. To maintain production Krupp made wide use of foreign slave labour and concentration camp inmates.

agriculture. Forced labour from Western Europe was usually sent to higher status industrial jobs.

Conditions for the labourers varied depending on employer and industry. Generally, skilled labour in factories received the best treatment while unskilled labour in mining, agriculture and building received the worst (although agricultural workers on small, isolated farms often received decent treatment from traditional farmers). Jewish or Slav peoples were almost invariably placed in sub-human conditions. A typical daily diet for them was two bowls of thin root-vegetable soup during the daytime, and a single hunk of bread in the evening. Once a week they might receive a small piece of meat.

Combined with long hours of work, this appalling diet resulted in chronic sickness and fatalities among workers.

The success of Nazi employment policies is demonstrated by the rise or maintenance of industrial output even up to the very last months of the war, even as German cities were gutted by Allied bombing. The German workforce produced 8295 military aircraft in 1939, 39,807 in 1944. Tank production was 27,300 vehicles in 1944, compared to 2200 in 1940. Steel output was 23.3 million tonnes (23.7 million tons) in 1939, 34 million tonnes (34.6 million tons) in 1943.

Such impressive levels of output are testimony in part to the intelligent policies of Albert Speer – who took over responsibility for

Above: Hitler (centre) at the launch of a battleship before World War II. The millions of tons of steel produced by German industry built him the ships, aircraft and tanks for his wars of conquest in Europe.

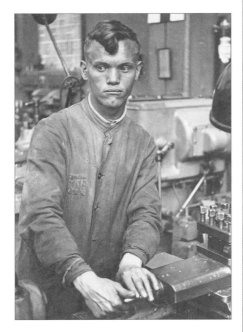

Germany's war production in 1942 – and the ruthless labour-acquisition polices of Fritz Sauckel, plenipotentiary for the mobilization of labour from the same year. But they also attest to the sheer resilience and loyalty of German labourers. Workers did receive an incentive to work after 1942 in the form of bonus payments for high productivity. However, the effect of this must have been increasingly minimal. Air raids over Germany's cities pushed many workers out into the countryside where the rates of pay were extremely depressed, often because German workers had to compete with unpaid foreign labour.

In late 1944 to 1945 the German economy, one of the most incredible labour phenomena in history, came crashing down. The Allies liberated the occupied territories, bombing decimated the German cities and millions of male workers found themselves conscripted into futile defence forces such as the *Volkssturm*. It was the end of an amazing economic journey. Robert Ley had once referred to the German workers as "soldiers of labour". Germany's

workforce had certainly built up the German nation ready for war. One of the principal reasons for Germany's defeat is that these labour combatants could not defeat the economic supremacy of the United States, which ultimately dwarfed German productivity. The sustained German production figures during the war demonstrate both the intense desire for victory and the rising, terrible, fear of defeat.

Above: Hitler's conquests in 1939–41 gave German industry a huge potential manpower pool. Workers were shipped in from France (above) and from Eastern Europe (top left).

141

Chapter 9
Minorities and genocide

National Socialist ideology sought to maintain the purity of the Aryan race, whose heartland lay among the Nordic peoples of Europe. Race enemies – the Jews, Slavs and other minority groups – had no future in the Thousand Year Reich.

In the summer of 1939, the eyes of the European world were centred on the crisis over Danzig. They were focused on the British and French guarantee to protect the sovereignty, if not the territorial integrity, of Poland. At this time, the Nazi Government began to murder disabled German children who were already in hospitals and asylums. These children were described as "life unworthy of life".

This deliberate state-directed and sponsored murder of some children was extended in September (coinciding with the invasion of Poland) to all German adults also described as "life unworthy of life". From then until August 1941 some 90,000 German citizens were systematically killed, mostly by carbon monoxide gas, in hospitals across Germany. These had been adapted with disguised gas chambers, as well as crematoria, to destroy the evidence. This treatment applied to patients who suffered from hereditary diseases, so described by the Nazis, whether physical or psychological. These included such ill-defined categories as "feeble-minded", schizophrenic

and even "a-social", all conditions that the Nazis considered made their sufferers totally unfit to be members of the *Volksgemeinschaft*. This whole operation was directed centrally from a suburban villa in Berlin, Tiergartenstrasse 4, which gave its codename T-4 to the operation. Philip Bouhler directed T-4 at the behest of Adolf Hitler. He had signed a specific authorization in October legitimizing the murders that had begun the previous month:

142

Above: The
apparatus of Nazi
mass murder –
concentration camp
crematoria for
disposing of the
remains of those who
had been gassed.

Berlin, 1 September 1939
Reich leader Bouhler ... charged with the
responsibility of enlarging the competence
of certain physicians ... so that patients
who, on the basis of human judgement,
are considered incurable, can be granted
mercy death after a discerning diagnosis.
(signed) A. Hitler.

On the basis of the euphemistic
language used here, this murder
programme was misleadingly called
the "Euthanasia campaign". In
essence it can be seen as an element
of a much larger programme that was
to be launched in 1941 against not
just the Jewish community of
Germany, but against all of Europe's
Jews. This was accompanied by a
swathe of other systematic killings: of
the "disabled" in Poland; and of
Europe's gypsies (Roma and Sinti).
These actions represented part of
what the Nazis neutrally called "The
Final Solution", but what the world
now knows as the Holocaust. It
involved the mass murder by the

Left: Malnourished
and exhausted, a Jew
wanders aimlessly in
the Warsaw Ghetto
in 1943. Between
1940 and 1942,
100,000 Jews died in
the ghetto.

Nazis and their allies of nearly six
million of Europe's Jews.

What, if any, is the link between
these two policies? How can this

143

unprecedented genocidal process be explained? The Holocaust marked a watershed not merely in European history, but also in world history. It sets the Nazi regime in a uniquely infamous position.

First of all, we need to understand the context. Germany's Jewish community comprised some 550,000 people, principally urban dwellers, concentrated in business occupations and the professions. Many were totally secularized, and all were living in the Reich with political, legal and economic rights guaranteed by the legislation introduced after 1869. Germany's Jews were emancipated citizens. This liberating process could not overcome all social pressures and prejudices, but it did mean that German Jewry was thoroughly integrated and intermarried within Germany's increasingly secularized society.

Anti-Semitism in late nineteenth-century Germany, as in much of Europe, had not only survived but acquired a more modern, if virulent, aspect of racist ideas and attitudes. As Hitler was to write in 1919: "Jewry is unqualifiedly a racial association not a religious association ... its influence will bring about the racial tuberculosis of the people." He added in a speech of 1920: "...and the deed remains irrevocably firm removal of the Jews from our nation, not because we would begrudge them their existence – we congratulate the rest of the world on their company – but because the existence of our own nation is a thousand times more important to us than that of an alien race." These ideas he had ingested in pre-1914 Vienna were to be incorporated into the Nazi Party programme. For Hitler himself they formed an essential part of his world view (*Weltanschauung*), a view in which he persisted right up to his death. As he wrote in his last political testament of 29 April 1945: "Above all I charge the leaders of the nation and those under them to scrupulous observance of the laws of race and to merciless opposition to the universal poisoner of all peoples, international Jewry."

In Hitler's mind the Jews constituted a unique and specific evil.

He saw them as a racial enemy to his supposed German master race. They were also seen as an ideological conspiracy operating behind world communism (or Bolshevism, as Hitler tended to call it) centred in the Soviet state, as well as being behind American capitalism. The contradictory nature of these ideas did not hamper Hitler's conviction of their rightness and importance. Once they were incorporated into the Nazi Party programme, one could only expect that they would lead to policies after the Nazis became part of the government in January 1933.

From January 1933 until September 1941, legal measures (enacted through central government decrees) and "extra legal" acts of random violence and local pressure (social, physical and economic) were imposed progressively on German Jewry. This was a process of incremental persecution designed to drive the Jews out of Germany, in pursuit of Hitler's goal of a Jew-free Germany (just as he had dreamed and spoken of in 1920).

To that end the Nazis pursued a series of policies in an often ill-coordinated way that was aimed at making life for Germany's Jews legally, socially and economically stressful and painful. They did this in the expectation that emigration would result. On 7 April 1933, it was deemed that "civil servants who are not of Aryan descent are to be retired". Then, on 11 April, "a person is to be considered non-Aryan if he is descended from non-Aryan and especially from Jewish parents or grandparents. It is sufficient if one parent or grandparent is Aryan."

Following Hitler's rabid rhetoric at that year's Nuremberg rally, the Reich Citizenship Law of 15 September 1935 was issued, together with the "Law for the protection of German Blood and German Honour". This forbade marriages

Below: The futility of protest. Jewish lawyer Michael Spiegel is marched barefoot through the streets of Munich. The placard reads: "I am a Jew but I will never again complain about the Nazis."

between Jews and Germans as well as extra-marital intercourse and, to foster the image of sexually predatory Jews, forbade the employment by Jews of female servants under 45 years old. A further gratuitous slap was administered to old Jewish soldiers and war veterans, forbidding them to fly the Reich flag or display the Reich colours as they customarily did.

To close possible loopholes, the First Regulation was issued on 14 November 1935. It stated:

A Jew cannot be a Reich citizen. He has no voting rights … He cannot occupy a public office. Jewish officials will retire as of 1 December 1935.

This 1935 decree became the baseline for definitions of Jews that was always referred to subsequently. More forceful measures followed in 1938–39. When Austria was taken over, anti-Semitic actions reached new heights. As Dr Leo Lauterbach reported back in London after a visit to Austria in April 1938: "This policy will be essentially different from that adopted in Germany and it may aim at a complete annihilation of Austrian Jewry."

Even this seemed to pale in relation to the violent events of the Nazi programme against Germany's Jews unleashed by Hitler and Goebbels on 9 and 10 November 1938 – *Kristallnacht*. The cold cynicism of leading Nazis is revealed in the secret instructional memorandum sent out by Reinhard Heydrich, Chief of the Reich Security Head Office, at 01:20 hours on 10 November 1938, in which the SD (*Sicherheitsdienst* – the party's own intelligence and security body) were instructed (with violence and burnings of synagogues already under way) that: "Places of business and apartments may be destroyed but not looted." And, crucially, "as many Jews … especially the rich … as can be

accommodated in existing prisons are to be arrested. After the detentions have been carried out the appropriate concentration camps are to be contacted immediately for the prompt accommodation of the Jews in the camps." This was aimed at some 30,000 male Jews. Their release was to be dependent on their agreeing to emigrate.

"Decisive steps" against the Jews

As a sequel, and in direct fulfilment of instructions from Hitler, Hermann Göring convened a meeting on 12 November at his Air Ministry headquarters to coordinate anti-Jewish policy through "decisive steps". The tone and attitude of the meeting is perfectly captured by Göring's remark revealed in the verbatim report of this meeting: "I would not want to be a Jew in Germany today." This was followed in 1939 by sustained attempts to completely remove Jews from the German economy in the hope that all would leave Germany entirely, creating the desired Jew-free state.

While not minimizing the suffering and distress, economic

Above: Hermann Göring, head of the *Luftwaffe*, who fully approved of the anti-Jewish *Kristallnacht* pogrom carried out in November 1938. After World War II he killed himself with cyanide the day before his execution.

then and later in the mounting extremism of Nazi anti-Jewish policies. The move to mass murder that began in 1941, and the decision to attempt to kill all of Europe's Jews, was to emerge out of a complex set of policies, events and decisions between September 1939 and December 1941. Especially important was the war against the Soviet Union from June 1941.

Germany's domestic moves against its own Jewish citizens cannot be detached from Nazi foreign policy. For while anti-Semitic policy was driven by the desire to hound all Jews out of the Reich, paradoxically German foreign policy and the idea of *Lebensraum* led to the expansion of the state into Austria (1938), the Sudetenland (1938) and the rest of Czechoslovakia (1939). In September 1939 the state expanded into Poland, followed by the moves in 1940 into France and Western Europe. Monumentally, June 1941 saw Operation Barbarossa against the Soviet Union. Each territorial move incorporated more and more Jews into the German empire. Some

Left: Reinhard Heydrich (left), anti-Semite, Chief of the Reich Security Office and organizer of the *Einsatzgruppen*. He is shown here in Prague Castle as the Protector of Bohemia and Moravia.

exploitation and despoliation – especially in Austria after March 1938 – official policy remained "emigration" of Jews, not murder. Austrian anti-Semitism exceeded anything seen up to that point in the Reich, and Austrian methods and personnel (for example, Adolf Eichmann) were to have a crucial role

Below: Heydrich's handiwork – a gutted synagogue in Magdeburg following *Kristallnacht*. In total 191 synagogues were set on fire, with a further 815 Jewish shops and 171 homes destroyed.

Left: German soldiers mock Jews in the Warsaw Ghetto. Those Jews who managed to survive living in the ghetto were eventually shipped off to the death camp at Treblinka to be gassed.

200,000 in Austria; approximately 3 million in Poland; and in Western Europe not only the Jewish citizens of the invaded states, but those refugees who had fled from earlier Nazi persecution. So Germany was simultaneously pursuing two incompatible ends. It considered the "Jewish Question" a problem, but, by its territorially expansionist wars, was driving that problem further and further from a solution.

The invasions of Poland and later the Soviet Union were to be central to the new, increasingly violent and ultimately murderous policies that would be pursued as a way out of this self-imposed dilemma. It was these policies that were to generate the full horrors of the Holocaust. When Poland was invaded in September 1939, behind the frontline troops came *Einsatzgruppen* (SS special action squads). Their tasks included the killing of Polish intellectuals and government officials, thus forestalling possible resistance. They would murder asylum patients to free hospitals, asylums and nursing homes for Nazi uses. They would also harass Polish Jews mercilessly.

This anti-Semitic strand of policy was extended further by directives from Heydrich and the new Governor General Hans Frank (now lording it over his new kingdom from Cracow Castle) ordering the creation of ghettos (so-called "Jewish residential districts") to concentrate Poland's already highly urbanized Jewish population into key urban areas, namely Lodz, Warsaw, Radom and Lublin. This was viewed as a temporary measure before some more permanent move "eastwards". Nazi policy was now concerned to drive Poland's Jews to remote eastern areas to free farms and urban premises for incoming "German" settlers, comprising a few from the Reich, but most from Latvia, Lithuania and eastern Poland – areas occupied by the Soviet Union in 1939. These eastern refugees, or *Volksdeutsche*, were to be settled in property and businesses taken from Jews and Poles who could expect to be dumped randomly under the brutal rule of Frank.

This process of "ghettoization" of Poland's Jews proceeded until autumn 1940 in a piecemeal, decentralized way that resulted in various ghettos and structures being created, the one in Warsaw being significantly different from that in Lodz. The Jews in these ghettos were subjected to marking with stars, and separation from the Poles as well as from the Germans. They were forced to exist in increasingly overcrowded, disease-ridden circumstances; and subjected to arbitrary bouts of forced labour while existing on ever-diminishing food rations. These Jews were precariously clinging to life while German ghetto administrators were confidently and callously imagining

Left: "One way or another – I will tell you quite openly – we must finish off the Jews." (Hans Frank, Governor General of Poland, December 1941). A dead child is taken away for burial in the Warsaw Ghetto.

Below: Inside the Warsaw Ghetto. The building is the headquarters of the *Judenrat*, the Jewish ruling council.

the "Jewish Question" would be "solved" in 8 to 10 years by "wastage". So the policy, while being conceived of as territorial, in practice was moving in an increasingly genocidal direction, though no such formal murderous central decision had yet been taken.

The war in Russia

Such a decision, or series of decisions, was to emerge out of Hitler's momentous idea to crown his 1939-40 military victories with the prized ultimate victory over the Soviet Union. This was a victory through war that the Führer thought would destroy not only the Soviet state but also Bolshevism – as well as striking a final blow against "International Jewry". For this campaign Hitler decreed a war quite unlike that pursued in Western Europe in 1940. This was to be a *Vernichtungskrieg* (a war of extermination). The nature of the violence, the attitudes to soldiers, prisoners of war, civilians and Jews was to be different. Space was to be cleared, and people destroyed by violence and starvation.

It is against this background and the decision to invade the Soviet Union that the comprehensively murderous approach to Russia's Jews and, subsequently, to all of Europe's Jews emerged. As in Poland, *Einsatzgruppen* were created. Some 3000 volunteers were specially trained to carry out murders behind the frontline of civilians. Initially aimed at killing "Commissars", local officials and mayors, the groups gradually extended their scope and killed male Jews. Then, in August and September 1941, they targeted whole Jewish communities, women and children included. This massive, murderous task now being undertaken in the East by Himmler, acting on Hitler's behalf, was beyond the original 3000 men of the *Einsatzgruppen*, so SS troops, police units, and foreign volunteers from Lithuania and the Ukraine were recruited to increase the number of full-time assassins.

A secret report from *Einsatzgruppe* A from October 1941 records that "large-scale executions were therefore carried out in the cities and

Above: Polish Jews about to be shot by members of an *Einsatzgruppe*, an SS special action squad. They were first organized by Himmler and Heydrich in 1939 to follow the armies into Poland.

countryside by *Sonderkommandos* [special units] … the work of the execution units was carried out smoothly. The total number of Jews liquidated in Lithuania is 71,105." A little later, Karl Jäger, the commander of *Einsatzkommando* 3, reported secretly to Berlin from Kovno (Kaunas):

I can confirm today that E3 has achieved the goal of solving the Jewish problem in Lithuania. There are no more Jews in Lithuania, apart from working Jews and their families. These number in Shavli, about 4500; in Kovno, about 15,000; in Vilna, about 15,000. I wanted to eliminate the working Jews and their families as well, but the civil administration and the Wehrmacht attacked me most sharply and issued a prohibition against having these Jews and their families shot.

There followed tabulated daily records of the tens of thousands who were shot between September and November 1941.

To this process of genocidal shooting was added experiments and trials of other killing methods, principally gas, which was designed to reduce the stress and strain on the killers. Thus, gassing of Russian POWs took place in August 1941, and experiments with gas vans were tried (the exhaust fumes were diverted into the enclosed rear of the vehicles crowded with victims).

While this process swept across the occupied Soviet Union, Poland's Jews remained incarcerated in the ghettos. They continued to be starved and overworked, and they approached with fear yet another bitter, malnourished winter. They were generally unaware of the even

Below: Forced to wear the Star of David, these Russian Jews were rounded up by the Germans to clean the streets.

greater threat that lay ahead. Equally, the remaining Jews of Germany, subjected to privations and arbitrary actions against them as they were, apparently remained even more distant from the murderous policy unfolding in the East.

Yet decisions had been made which would tragically link together the fate of all these different Jewish communities. In July 1941, Göring had sent a memo to Heydrich calling for an "outline plan for the Final Solution of the Jewish question in Europe". In August, the formal ending of the Euthanasia programme, following public protests, led to the redirection east into Poland of many

of the "gassing" experts and technicians for reasons as yet unspecified. In September, Germany's Jews were required for the first time to wear, like their brethren in the East, a Star of David. In October they were forbidden to leave the Reich. They were now marked and trapped.

This process of demarcation and closing avenues of escape had come about in response to a series of decisions that had been taken at the highest level. For, in October and November, preliminary work was begun on a "camp" at Belzec on the Lublin–Lvov railway line. This process was to lead to the creation of Germany's "factories of death" which would operate from early 1942 at Belzec, Sobibor and Treblinka. In November, Heydrich, following Göring's authorization, sent out invitations to senior administrators to convene for a meeting in early December. The invitations received by the 15 men were accompanied by a copy of Göring's memorandum of 31 July 1941 about the Final Solution (*Endlösung*). These desk-bound murderers were to coordinate with some of the *Einsatzgruppen* killers from the East to ensure the smooth operation of a total programme of extermination.

Their deliberations were disrupted by the Japanese attack on Pearl Harbor (7 December 1941) and the

subsequent decision by Hitler to
declare war on the US. Heydrich and
his associates arranged to reconvene
their meeting on 20 January 1942, at
the lakeside villa of Wannsee in the
plush Berlin suburb of the same
name. However, even before their
deliberations got under way, gas vans
operating at Chelmno began to kill
Jewish victims brought from the
Lodz ghetto. What this meeting did
was to bring together the crucial
administrators across the German
bureaucratic machine to link them
with the soon-to-be-opened killing
centres in Poland. This meant that
the decisions from earlier in 1941
could be implemented.

The Wannsee Conference

They targeted Europe's 11 million
Jews, carefully catalogued and listed
by Heydrich's assistant, Adolf
Eichmann, who kept the minutes for
the meeting. These minutes provide a
substantial record of Nazi thinking
and intentions, all couched in
euphemistic Nazi-speak, where
"evacuation" means killing. This
Wannsee Conference ensured the
linking of the administrative machine
to German industry to produce
Zyklon B (a commercial gas based on

prussic acid) for Auschwitz; to
German railways to transport the
victims from all over Europe to
Poland; to the SS and SD personnel
as perpetrators; and to the banks and
auction houses to seize and sell
Jewish property. For the first time in
history, a modern industrial state
sought to harness all the resources
and methods usually associated with
production exclusively to serve the
ends of murder and death.

As a consequence of this meeting,
in the spring and summer of 1942 the
Jews of Poland began to be brutally
torn from the ghettos, where
hundreds of thousands had survived
for up to 30 months. These ghetto
inhabitants were barely able to
conceive of what had been prepared
for them by the Nazis under the
codename Operation Reinhardt.

Take the example of Warsaw. The
great clearance began in July 1942 as
the Nazis set about "evacuating"
Warsaw's Jews to the East. In fact,
they were going to the newly created
death camp at Treblinka. Adam
Czerniakow, the head of the *Judenrat*
(Jewish council), was instructed to
ensure that 6000 Jews assembled at
the railway station on 22 July 1942
and that this would be the "minimum

daily quota". Czerniakow committed suicide rather than comply, but the deportations proceeded. Over the next year the camp at Treblinka murdered some 700,000 Polish Jews, including around 400,000 from the Warsaw ghetto.

Simultaneously, Belzec and Sobibor were receiving and killing Jews from other Polish ghettos, probably doubling the total murdered at Treblinka. All the while the mass shootings continued in western Russia as they had since the autumn of 1941. Finally, the great prison labour and concentration camp complex at Auschwitz in southern Poland had purpose-built killing facilities added. Large gas chambers and specially commissioned crematoria were built to dispose of the corpses. German industrialists competed keenly for such contracts, the embossed plates on the furnaces a solid testament to their manufacturers' pride.

From late 1941 this destruction process began to engulf Germany's Jews. An early train of "evacuees" was sent to Riga in Latvia where they were shot on arrival. As 1942 advanced, Germany's Jews were swept into the Holocaust that had earlier engulfed Russian and Polish Jews. While the fundamental victims of the evolving murder programme were Europe's Jews, it had initially (as has been described earlier) engulfed Germany's disabled population. But another minority was to be stigmatized and maltreated by the Nazis. This was Germany's gypsy (Roma and Sinti) population. To these traditionally migrant family and clan groups the Nazis showed a mixture of traditional prejudices, stereotypically viewing them as criminal, work-shy and troublemakers. To this they added "newer" attitudes, regarding the gypsies as racially inferior. As a consequence, Nazi policy towards gypsies displayed an erratic course, trying to blend early aims to force wanderers to settle with hostile local objections to such settlements.

Between 1933 and 1937, central and local authorities intensified measures of both control and harassment. The period 1937–38 saw an intensification of the criminalization of gypsies. Crime prevention was stressed as a justification for preventive custody in

Below: Austrian gypsies about to be deported to a camp in 1938. In general, the Nazis viewed the gypsies as an inferior race, and it is estimated that up to 90,000 were killed by them during World War II.

concentration camps being imposed arbitrarily on male gypsies. This took on an even more sinister and overtly racial dimension with Himmler's 1938 decree, "Fight against the Gypsy Plague". This was a particular preoccupation of Himmler's in which Hitler had no direct interest. Gypsies are not mentioned in *Mein Kampf*, and beyond a few subsequent comments and remarks he allowed Himmler to proceed as he thought best in a rather disorderly way against the gypsies.

The fate of the gypsies

Once the war had begun, especially after 1941, gypsies in Eastern Europe became victims of *Einsatzgruppen* squads, army groups (especially in Serbia), SS and police units as they massacred civilians deemed "dangerous" as part of the war against the Soviet Union. By 1941 there were perhaps 26,000 gypsies in Germany and Austria. Some 2500 of these had been sent to the General Government of Poland in May 1940, and a further 5000 were sent directly to the Lodz ghetto in October and November 1941. There, subjected to massive privations, many succumbed to typhus; and, after gassings had begun in December 1941 (at Chelmno-Kulmhof), some 4400 of these gypsies perished in vans there.

Himmler's next major step was his deportation order of 16 December 1942 aimed at despatching all "a-social" gypsies to Auschwitz. While this order allowed for many exemptions among so-called "pure" gypsies and "good" mixed gypsies, German local authorities were all too keen to clear their own regions to heed the restraining niceties of such distinctions. In March 1943, for example, as a consequence, some 13,000 German gypsies were deported to Auschwitz where they were lodged in a special section known as the "gypsy family camp". There they remained in groups, suffering terribly from disease and malnutrition but not being systematically murdered until 1944, when the gypsy camp was going to be swamped temporarily by the hundreds of thousands of incoming Hungarian Jews who were to be gassed there from 16 May 1944 onwards.

All told, probably 22,000 of Germany's 29,000 gypsies were killed by Nazi policies. Michael Zimmermann, a leading German expert on the Roma and Sinti, claims that probably more than 90,000 gypsies across Europe were killed by the Nazis and their allies. One aspect that distinguishes the Nazi murder of the gypsies from that of the Jews is revealed in the following paradox. In the Nazi view, gypsy *Mischlinge* (mixed race) were the real enemy, while pure gypsies were often treated less violently; for Jews, it was the other way round. "Pure" Jews were seen as the ultimate evil and could

expect nothing but death; *Mischlinge* were viewed more inconsistently.

Germany's blacks and gays

While not necessarily targeted for murder, two other groups were the victims not of their beliefs or actions (such as the communists, socialists or Jehovah's Witnesses), but for who or what they were. These were Germany's homosexuals and the minority "black" population, offspring of the African colonial troops who occupied defeated Germany after 1919. Those whom Hitler denigrated in *Mein Kampf* as the "10,000 black bastards of the Rhine" were subjected to forcible sterilization (as well as significant social stigmatization). The reaction to gays was more complex, being homophobia mixed with arguments from Himmler about failing to procreate and make good those of the national community lost in World War I. The consequences for gays ranged from imprisonment; "curative" and barbaric medical treatment; and, later, being forced into concentration camps, where the wearers of the pink triangle were regular victims of sadistic guards and brutal criminal inmates.

For all its claims about ending class divisions and creating an organic, wholesome society, the Nazi *Volksgemeinschaft* was rather more marked by the brutal and murderous policies inflicted on those excluded from that utopian goal. While violence, imprisonment and destruction were often visited on minority groups within and beyond the Reich between 1933 and 1945, it was Europe's Jews who were a specific and peculiarly distinctive target. On racial and ideological grounds they were singled out for destruction in a process that unfolded consistently from 1941 onwards. Non-Jewish Poles were murdered and killed in large numbers (approximately three million from 1939 to 1945). Russian civilians and POWs were murdered or starved to death in huge numbers, but the intention was never to kill all Poles or all of Russia's citizens. However, this was precisely the plan for Europe's Jews. All were to be killed. This was an historically unprecedented process whereby a whole group, designated by who and what they were considered to be, was to be destroyed totally. Genocidal policies were to be extended to a qualitatively distinctive extent, deploying novel means of mass destruction in purpose-built factories of death which were then to be dismantled (as was done at Belzec, Sobibor and Treblinka in 1943), when their purpose had been achieved. Poland's Jews had been destroyed. Only the Allied victory and German defeat was to forestall the Nazi attempt to kill all of Europe's Jews.

Above: Gypsies in an Austrian concentration camp (left) and on their way to a camp (right). Ironically, though they persecuted them, the Nazis never considered gypsies enemies of the state.

157

Chapter 10
The army and military service

Though largely aloof from politics in the 1920s, during the 1930s the army was thoroughly indoctrinated with Nazi ideology. These beliefs were embraced with enthusiasm by the army, and were to have terrible consequences during World War II.

During the years of the Weimar Republic, the German Army had prided itself on being an institution above politics. The army, it was said, had no political affiliation and served no particular party. That said, the armed forces had major grievances over the conditions of the Treaty of Versailles imposed on Germany. Following the defeat of Imperial Germany in World War I and the foundation of the Weimar Republic, the *Vorläufige Reichswehr* (Provisional Army) was formed on 6 March 1919 from the remains of the old Imperial forces. It was made up of 43 brigades, which went down to 20 brigades when it was restructured into the *Übergangsheer* (Transitional Army) on 1 October 1919. In October 1920 the army was again reduced, to 100,000 men, as stipulated by the Versailles Treaty. The name of the army was changed once again, on 1 January 1921, to *Reichsheer* (National Army). The *Reichswehr* included the *Reichsheer* and the *Reichsmarine* (National Navy), and was replaced by the *Wehrmacht* (armed forces) on 20 May 1935. Given the right-wing

Below: An artillery unit of the 100,000-strong German Army on exercise on the outskirts of Berlin in 1924.

Below right: German infantry on manoeuvres in 1926. Though small, the army contained an excellent officer corps and soldiery.

sympathies and nationalist views held by most of the *Reichswehr*'s officer corps, this claim to stand above parties – the alleged *Überparteilichkeit* – was something of an exaggeration. It is true that, in the 1920s, the army as an institution did not as a rule interfere in politics. In return, the politicians granted the army considerable autonomy to run its own affairs. This deliberately separate relationship between army and state was to experience a total transformation once the Nazi Party

Above: German recruits learn how to goose-step in 1937. By this date Hitler had introduced rearmament and conscription.

came to power in January 1933. Very quickly thereafter, the army discovered that, willingly or otherwise, it was to become the subservient instrument of the National Socialist regime.

Given the nature of the Nazi state, it is hardly surprising that Hitler and his followers should have wanted to control the military. In part, this was sheer pragmatism. The Nazi Party was a totalitarian organization that believed in the supreme authority of its leader (the so-called *Führerprinzip*). It could hardly tolerate an independent military, given that such a body had the ability to challenge National Socialist rule, if necessary by force. Ensuring the army's loyalty, and thereby neutralizing the one organization that could strip the party of power, was an essential prerequisite to the regime's long-term survival.

In addition, there were ideological considerations that necessitated wide-ranging interference in military affairs. Hitler, as we have seen in previous chapters, was driven by his belief in the superiority of the German people over all other races.

This doctrine, which would be used to justify brutal and genocidal policies inside Germany against the country's minority populations, would also be used by Hitler as the rationale for his external goal of conquering Europe in order to provide "living space" for the German Reich. Given that the land Hitler sought was populated by other nationalities, its acquisition for German settlement (an outcome dependent on conquest, followed by the expulsion or murder of the existing population) could only be effected by naked aggression and brute force. To achieve this, Hitler needed not only a large and capable army, but one that shared his agenda and was willing to carry out his cruel and inhuman plans without conscience. An army that stressed beliefs about political neutrality and which might be squeamish about breaching international conventions concerning the laws and customs of war, was of no use to him. He needed one that was driven explicitly by Nazi doctrines and was willing to put these into practice irrespective of all other, especially moral, considerations.

Above: The pre-Nazi German Army training for mechanized warfare. Though the dummy tanks may look comical, such exercises laid the foundation for the panzer divisions that were formed later.

For diverse reasons, Hitler came to power intent on forming an army that would be characterized by its obedience to the regime; by its sincere adoption of Nazi ideology, including its most brutal and racist elements; and by its effectiveness as a vehicle for conquest. The creation of such a military establishment would have major implications for the future character of the *Wehrmacht*, as the *Reichswehr* was now called. To become a truly National Socialist institution, it would have to shed its *Überparteilich* beliefs and undergo an extensive period of political re-orientation and indoctrination. The institution that emerged from such a process was unlikely to resemble the one that existed at its start.

In a similar fashion, the creation of such a military establishment would also have major implications for the ordinary German citizen. This was because an army of sufficient size and power to be capable of conquering Europe could only be created by conscription. As a result, the rise to power of the Nazis and the implementation of their foreign policy agenda entailed a social revolution for many Germans. People who might otherwise have spent their entire lives without having anything to do with the army would now find their existence shaped by the experience of compulsory military service, reintroduced in Germany in March 1935.

Hitler's army

Taken individually, the transformation of the army into a true National Socialist institution and the reintroduction of conscription were each highly significant developments. Taken together, they were of even more importance. The result of their near simultaneous occurrence was that, from this point, military training in a doctrinaire National Socialist environment became a fact of life for the vast majority of young German males. Their experience of this process would shape both how they behaved

Below: The Nazis reaped the rewards of the work done on mechanized warfare in the 1920s. Here, Adolf Hitler (in the first car, seated next to the driver) reviews a line of Panzer I tanks on the occasion of his birthday.

as individuals and how the *Wehrmacht* conducted itself as a body. It is to these developments that we now turn.

The army's oath to Hitler

While conscription and political re-orientation were of equal significance for the creation of the army that Hitler desired, it was the latter process, the transformation of the *Wehrmacht* into a loyal National Socialist institution, that was first to get under way. Given the magnitude of the changes involved, the process was surprisingly rapid. The first sign of this metamorphosis came in February 1934 when the swastika, the National Socialist Party emblem and the symbol of the new regime, was adopted as part of the army's insignia. By an order of the high command it

was incorporated into military badges, colours and uniforms. Six months later, this was followed by the introduction of a new military oath of allegiance. In place of the Weimar vow, which had required soldiers to pledge their "loyalty to the constitution" and to "be obedient to the President", a new formula was introduced that required German servicemen to declare their unfettered fealty to Adolf Hitler. The text ran simply:

I swear by God this holy oath, that I will render to Adolf Hitler, Führer of the German Reich and People, Supreme Commander of the Armed Forces, unconditional obedience, and that I am ready as a brave soldier to risk my life at any time for this oath.

Above: National Party Day, 1937. Police units march past the Führer. Many of the new units in the rearmed German Army were raised from the police, which was a paramilitary organization.

It is possible to exaggerate the importance of these words. They did not, for example, make German troops honour-bound to carry out war crimes if ordered to do so, an excuse that would later be used by many of those charged after the war with breaches of international law. Nevertheless, the new oath was still highly symbolic. Like the adoption of the Nazi Party insignia, it provided a very visible outward indication of the army's abandonment of its old *Überparteilich* ideals and served as a clear and unambiguous testament to its chosen identification with the new National Socialist order. What, after all, could be clearer than a pledge of blind loyalty to the leader of the Nazi movement itself?

An Aryan army

The army did not confine itself to symbolic changes. In incremental stages, it also began to conform to Nazi ideology. One of the most significant indications of this was the army's decision to enforce the party's discriminatory racial doctrines. Thus, in February 1934, General Werner von Blomberg, the Minister for War (who viewed Hitler as a strong man who would restore Germany's greatness), decided on his own authority and with no prompting from Hitler to institute racial restrictions on military appointments by incorporating the "Aryan Paragraph" into the *Wehrmacht*'s procedures. As a result, 50 members of the armed forces were discharged from the service on account of their Jewish background. This ban on Jewish soldiers was only the start. In December of the same year a decree was issued by General Werner von Fritsch, the Commander-in-Chief of the Army, prohibiting military personnel from taking Jewish wives. "It must be a matter of course," the decree stated, "that an officer seeks his wife only in the Aryan groups of the nation."

What applied to matrimony was soon also applied to shopping. In July 1935 von Blomberg ordered soldiers neither to frequent nor to patronize Jewish retailers. "It conflicts with the duty of the *Wehrmacht* as one of the responsible schools of the new state," he informed the army in an official decree, "when soldiers shop in non-Aryan businesses."

At one level, these regulations were petty acts of no real significance. There were, after all, not that many Jewish soldiers, few Jews were married to military personnel, and Jewish shopkeepers could survive without the patronage of members of the army. In short, the inconvenience caused by these infantile and bigoted decisions was very limited. However, these measures sent out a very clear signal. The army, it was clearly being stated, was an Aryan army because it was a National Socialist army. Moreover, it was an army that believed in the doctrine of racial purity and was willing, even desirous, of doing its bit to further this aim. As we shall see, with the re-introduction of conscription, this message would be transmitted wholesale to the millions of men who passed through the army's ranks, with terrible consequences.

Plans for expansion

From the above, it is evident that in the first few years after the Nazi seizure of power, the army deliberately remodelled itself on National Socialist lines. To this end, it adopted party insignia, swore devotion to the Nazi leader, and accepted the NSDAP's creed, even down to its most vulgar and bigoted racial doctrines. Most significantly, it did all this willingly and with conviction, because, as War Minister von Blomberg made clear in a decree issued in May 1934, the principles of the Nazi Party and those of the army were one and the same. As he put it:

National Socialism draws its rule of conduct from the necessities of the life of the whole people, and from the duty to work in concert for the entire nation. It embraces the idea of the fellowship of blood, of the fate of all German people. It is indubitable that this principle is, and must also remain, the foundation of the duty of the German soldier...

No one statement could have made it clearer that Hitler had succeeded in his objective of creating an obedient and loyal National Socialist army. However, as was made evident at the outset, this was not his only goal for the *Wehrmacht*. It was also his intention to turn it into a large army.

When Hitler came to power in January 1933, two obstacles stood in the way of such a military expansion. First of all, the size of the German armed forces was strictly limited by international agreement. Under the Treaty of Versailles signed, unwillingly, by Germany after her defeat in World War I, the military was prohibited from having more than 100,000 serving officers and men. To go above this figure would

technically be a breach of international law that many in Germany feared might invite retaliation from the other powers. Therefore, until the attitude of the Reich's neighbours was known, it was generally felt better that rearmament be undertaken cautiously, surreptitiously and with care.

German rearmament

The second problem was that, in 1933, the Reich simply did not possess the necessary military infrastructure (barracks, parade grounds, canteens, training personnel, uniforms, etc) to accommodate a large increase in numbers. Without such facilities, all the reintroduction of conscription would have achieved would have been the calling up of men. These would have been impossible to clothe, house, arm, feed or train, so there was little point in doing it. All that would have resulted from such a measure would have been chaos.

As a result, in its initial stages, German rearmament was managed carefully both to avoid antagonizing

Above: Von Blomberg (centre) presents standards to *Wehrmacht* units. Behind him stands army commander-in-chief General Freiherr Werner von Fritsch, another officer who supported the Nazis.

Opposite: Hitler (centre) with War Minister von Blomberg (gesturing with hand) at an armaments exhibition in 1937. He set an example to the army by taking an oath of loyalty to Hitler in person.

Left: German 18-year-old recruits wait to be lectured in National Socialist ideology, 1938. Such indoctrination ensured a pro-Nazi German Army.

Below: Hitler Youth boys in 1937. Members were continually exposed to Nazi ideology, thus creating the perfect material for the army.

other countries and to minimize possible disruption either to the army or to the nation. To this end, many of the new recruits were chosen from people who had some sort of existing military experience. For example, in 1934 and 1935, many of the new *Wehrmacht* formations were raised from the ranks of the police, especially the *Landespolizei* and the *Schutzpolizei*, whose members had been receiving basic military training since the early 1920s to enable them to cope with "serious civil disturbances". The transition from service in a paramilitary organization to membership of a fully military organization not being such a major one, most of these former *Landespolizei* constables adapted quickly and easily to their new status as soldiers.

Such action was indicative of the manner in which the army gained personnel in the first years of the Nazi regime. However, in March 1935, Hitler decided that he had

waited long enough and that it was time to re-introduce conscription. The advantages of the two-year delay were apparent in the foreign policy sphere. Despite all the fears, there was no meaningful retaliation by the other powers. Germany's diplomats had clearly laid the groundwork well. In domestic terms, the delay also reaped dividends as the time had been devoted to creating the necessary basic facilities for housing and training the new recruits. Thus conscription, while certainly testing the army's resources to the limit, would not push them past breaking point, as would have been the case in 1933. Most importantly, two years of Nazi rule also meant that the army was now able to draw an increasing proportion of its 18-year-old recruits from people who had spent their formative years being inculcated into a military culture through membership of the Hitler Youth (HJ). This body, through its hierarchical structure and paramilitary

Above: German soldiers with a captured Russian on the Eastern Front. Their exposure to Nazi ideology meant they would regard him as sub-human.

organization, did much to ready Germany's youth for military life. Even more significantly, it also exposed them to a continuous stream of National Socialist ideas. As a result, former HJ members constituted the perfect human material for the fervently Nazi army that Hitler intended to create.

The army and Nazi ideology

Nothing would be left to chance. The programme of National Socialist indoctrination that these youths had received in the HJ would continue after they were enlisted in the army. Indeed, despite many myths to the contrary, constant exposure to Nazi ideology would prove one of the defining features of army life for the nation's conscripts. This was quite deliberate. As War Minister von Blomberg explained in a decree of 16 April 1935:

With the introduction of general conscription, the Armed Forces again became the great school of National education. Several times Adolf Hitler has stressed the importance of this task. On 1 May 1934, he gave the Army the task of being ... "a national and social melting pot for the education of a new German human being". In his book, "Mein Kampf", the significance of the Armed Forces for the education of the people is often emphasized ... In other places, the Führer designates the completion of military service as the prerequisite for the granting of the rights of citizenship. Service in the Armed Forces is therefore the last and highest step in the course of the general education of a young German, from parental home, through school, Hitler Youth, and the Labour Service. The educational goal of the Wehrmacht *is not only the basically trained soldier and the master of a weapon, but also the man who is aware of his nationality and of his general duties towards the state.*

Above: Erich von Manstein, one of the great German strategists of World War II. As commander of the Eleventh Army in Russia, he exhorted his men to show no mercy towards Jews and Bolsheviks.

Great efforts were made to put this programme of political education into practice. Beginning in 1936, courses were introduced at the *Wehrmacht* Academy, the Staff College and at the principal officer training establishments to school commanders in the art of political instruction. Run by party propaganda specialists, these courses were designed to ensure that the local military leadership possessed the necessary skills and ability to run weekly political education sessions for their men, in which a heavy diet of National Socialist propaganda could be disseminated. To reinforce this, the party also provided the armed forces with a wealth of written propaganda material. Instructional booklets, leaflets and brochures on the principles of Nazism, for example, were widely distributed among the troops. So, too, were copies of the main party newspaper, the *Völkischer Beobachter*, which was issued to the army at government expense.

Even more importantly, the rank and file was also exposed to an endless stream of speeches and radio broadcasts, all designed to solidify their adherence to the party's message. No effort was spared to ensure the effectiveness of these measures. The speeches were often grand occasions. Johannes Steinhoff, an officer cadet in the *Luftwaffe*, recalled that when, in 1936, Hermann Göring came to speak to his graduating class, all of them (up to 1000 newly commissioned lieutenants) were assembled in the splendour of the Prussian Parliament building. The imposing setting, along with a dynamic speech, left a marked impression. As Steinhoff later recalled:

Göring spoke for about an hour. His behaviour was theatrical. He used popular terms, speaking of disgrace, humiliation, the Reich's right to "living space", and he promised retaliation. When he closed with "and you will one day be my vengeance", there probably wasn't a single person in attendance who wasn't totally motivated to give his utmost in support of this regime.

The barrage of propaganda directed at the rank and file of the *Wehrmacht* may have taken various forms, but its message was fundamentally always the same. The soldiers were fed repeatedly a rabid diet of racist dogma that held up the Aryan German nation as the ideal community and, at the same time, demonized other peoples, especially the Jews and the Bolshevik Russians,

as Germany's principal enemies. Additionally, the soldiers were constantly told of the Reich's need for expansion. Germany, it was said, lacked a viable living space, a situation that could only be remedied by seizing land from "inferior" peoples. Finally, the soldiers were continually led to believe that, in Adolf Hitler, they had a leader of superhuman, almost divine, genius, who would lead them to unparalleled future greatness and whose inspired commands had to be followed at all costs. This mixture of mutually reinforcing ideas, spread constantly among the ranks, would have had a huge impact on the character of the *Wehrmacht*. Just what that impact would be would become clear only with the outbreak of war – especially

Below: General Walter von Reichenau, who during the campaign in Russia issued orders that sanctioned the killing of Russians and Jews. He died of a stroke in 1942.

the war on the Eastern Front from June 1941.

The attack that was launched by Germany against the Soviet Union in June 1941 unleashed a war like no other before it. It entailed brutality without comparison. Contrary to the myth often propagated by apologists for the German Army, much of this brutality was perpetrated by the *Wehrmacht*. Studied from various perspectives, this is hardly surprising. As the recipients of years of racist propaganda, German soldiers were quite naturally prone to regard the Russian peoples as primitive *Untermenschen* (sub-humans), whose lives were of no consequence. This was a viewpoint that was hardly likely to lead to them treating the conquered population with consideration. Moreover, this racist mindset was specifically and deliberately reinforced both before

the launch of Operation Barbarossa, and during the early days of the German attack by explicit declarations from the army leadership. On 10 October 1941 General Walter von Reichenau, commander of the Sixth Army, informed his troops:

The essential goal of the campaign against the Jewish-Bolshevik system is the complete destruction of its power instruments and the eradication of the Asiatic influence on the European cultural sphere. Thereby the troops have tasks, which go beyond the conventional soldierly tradition. In the East the soldier is not only a fighter according to the rules of warfare, but also a carrier of an inexorable racial conception and the avenger of all the bestialities which have been committed against the Germans and related races. Therefore the soldier must have complete understanding for the

Below: An estimated 25,000 Russian prisoners taken during the capture of Sevastopol in Russia, 1942. German racial policy would result in most of these captives dying from starvation, forced labour or disease.

necessity of the harsh, but just atonement of Jewish sub-humanity.

Von Reichenau (who, had he not died of a stroke in 1942, would undoubtedly have been prosecuted for war crimes by the Allies) was not alone in attempting to incite racially motivated brutality. The highly respected strategist General Erich von Manstein called on the soldiers of his Eleventh Army to behave in a like manner. "The Jewish-Bolshevik system," he informed his troops, "must be eradicated once and for all." To this end, he entreated his unit to "show understanding for the harsh atonement of Judaism, the spiritual carrier of the Bolshevik terror".

Encouraged both by years of propaganda and by the recent exhortations of their commanders to view the Russians as primitive *untermenschen* unworthy of life, many German soldiers did just that. The most vivid testimony to the

Above: POWs taken by the Germans on the Eastern Front were rarely given food or water. These Russian prisoners are drinking stagnant water, which has collected in a shell crater, in order to quench their thirst.

Left: A Russian partisan taken prisoner by the Germans on the Eastern Front. German Army savagery in Russia was responsible for swelling partisan ranks, especially reprisal actions.

prevalence of these sentiments comes from the opinions expressed in the letters written by frontline soldiers in the East to their loved ones back in Germany. The vocabulary used to describe the Russian people was anything but flattering. One lance-corporal, for example, described them as "the most depraved and filthiest [people] living on God's earth", while another soldier described the Russians as "scoundrels, the scum of the earth", and went on to comment, "Can you imagine that human beings grow up like animals?". These bigoted statements were by no means atypical of the opinions that were expressed. If anything they were among the more moderate statements. One private described the Russians as "beasts" and then went on to suggest that "for them even the most horrible death is still too good". Another soldier expressed his satisfaction at being on the Russian Front and thus having the chance "to eradicate this universal plague".

Unfortunately, the attack on Russia gave these soldiers the opportunity to put these views into practice. All too predictably, given the chance to commit atrocities against a despised population, many German soldiers did just that. This took many forms. One of the most common was the "wild requisitioning" at gunpoint of food and property from Soviet citizens by German soldiers. Justified as a form of living off the land, this policy was carried to such an extreme that it became little more than armed robbery. Moreover, it had devastating effects on the civilian population, as the German records themselves clearly show. A report from the 12th Infantry Division, for example, recorded that "the land was exploited to the utmost ... Thereby a situation of general lack of food supplies for the civilian population arose, which in some cases caused starving Russian civilians to turn to German units and ask for relief or beg to be shot."

Russian civilians were often shot, hanged or murdered by other means. The *Wehrmacht* employed a system of collective punishment in which the many were made to suffer for the

Above: A Russian village is burnt by German troops in reprisal for a partisan attack. Often the inhabitants would also be executed.

Top right: "We are engaged in a primitive ... racial battle." (Himmler) SS troops round up suspected partisans in Russia.

Bottom right: Consequences of an ideology – execution of "sub-human" Russians by the SS. Public hangings were considered good deterrents.

The sign reads:

Wir sind Partisanen
und haben auf deutsche
Soldaten geschossen

Мы партизаны, —
стрелявшие по
ГЕРМАНСКИМ
ВОЙСКАМ

behaviour, real or imagined, of the few. A single act of resistance by one person could lead to the execution of an entire village. Resistance was very broadly defined. It could, for example, include feeding a Russian soldier. Such reprisal attacks were mostly out of all proportion to the alleged crime. In December 1941, on the basis of guerrilla activity in which six Germans died, troops from II Corps torched 16 villages and killed 448 people.

Another deprivation inflicted on the Russian population was forced labour. This was organized in a particularly brutal manner. Those who were conscripted ended up as little more than slaves, forced to undertake back-breaking work with inadequate rations. Countless of these unfortunates were worked to death and starved to death simultaneously. They were often luckier than those deemed "useless" for such labour, many of whom were driven from their homes. Given the severity of the Russian climate, where temperatures could reach 40 degrees below

freezing in winter, it is clear that the victims of such "evacuations" were often being given a death sentence. A similar fate befell any of those unlucky enough to live in an area from which the German Army decided to retreat. Instructed to follow a scorched earth policy, German soldiers torched entire villages, taking the young men for labour service and sending the elderly, the women and the children off into the frozen wilderness.

Still worse was the treatment of prisoners of war. Many, there is evidence to suggest, were shot out of hand by German soldiers, often on the flimsy justification that they were captured "partisans". So extensive was this arbitrary shooting that some commanders attempted to intervene. Sometimes this was on moral grounds, but more often than not it was based on the pragmatic consideration that "the ultimate result of the maltreatment or shooting of POWs after they had given themselves up in battle would be ... a stiffening of the enemy's

Above: "In battle, our troops can do as they please: hang partisans, even hang them head down or quarter them." Alfred Jodl, Chief of *Wehrmacht* operations, who was hanged by the Allies in 1946.

resistance, because every Red Army soldier fears German captivity". This was undoubtedly correct but, as little was done to enforce such orders, the shootings and maltreatment continued with exactly the consequences described.

Those POWs not killed had little to look forward to. If they were wounded, it was unlikely that they would receive medical treatment, which had been expressly prohibited. This meant they would either recover on their own or, more likely, waste away and die. If they survived, they could expect to receive minimal rations, but be required to undertake hard labour for their captors. As with Russian civilians, this often meant being worked to death in support of the *Wehrmacht*. Ironically, if they survived the war an uncertain fate awaited them, for Stalin believed that those who allowed themselves to fall into enemy hands were traitors.

The actions of the German Army on the Eastern Front were often far from honourable. While it would be wrong to brand all soldiers criminals, as there were clearly many upright men in the *Wehrmacht*, atrocities of various kinds were committed against Soviet soldiers and civilians alike. The reason for this, as the historian Omer Bartov has demonstrated conclusively, is that the *Überparteilich* German Army of the 1920s became Hitler's army in the 1930s and 1940s. Ideologically and politically reliable, and believing fully in the genius of their leader, German soldiers attempted to put Nazi doctrines about German racial supremacy and the need for *Lebensraum* into practice in the Eastern theatre of war. The consequence was that, for many Germans, the experience of national service was the experience of a brutal war, fought in a bestial manner in inhospitable conditions. As a former member of the élite *Grossdeutschland* Division recorded, in such circumstances "man becomes an animal". Many German soldiers succumbed to this transformation, and this quotation is perhaps the most fitting epitaph for the army that Hitler created.

Above: Hitler reviews German Army troops. The army's total commitment to Nazi ideology resulted in a brutal war in Russia, a war in which it committed countless atrocities but which led to its destruction.

Chapter 11
Wartime policies and privations

During the first two years of World War II the living standards of ordinary Germans remained high. However, they began to decline from 1941 as the war in Russia sucked up more and more resources, and as Germany was pounded from the air by bombers.

While the German population greeted the outbreak of war in September 1939 with considerable trepidation, the conflict at its onset made much less difference to most people's lives than might have been expected. There were three main reasons. To begin with, when Great Britain and France declared war on Germany, they did so without any real sense of how they would prosecute such an undertaking. As a result, in the opening months of the conflict they did very little to turn their declaration of war into a reality. No offensive operations took place and, in the absence of any meaningful attacks on German territory, it became, to use the parlance of the period, a "phoney war" or *Sitzkrieg*

(sitting down warfare). For much of the time, there was so little fighting that ordinary Germans could have been forgiven for not realizing there was a war going on at all.

Secondly, and also contributing to the sense of continued normality, economic conditions on the German home front did not alter radically in the first months of the war. It has been claimed that this stability occurred because Hitler chose deliberately to wage war in a manner that placed only the most limited demands on the civilian population. By adopting a *Blitzkrieg* (lightning warfare) military strategy of rapid and victorious campaigns, it has been said, he was able to pursue a *Blitzkrieg* economic strategy that did not require the full mobilization of the country's economy for "total war".

An economy geared for war

The actual reason for the apparent continuity of domestic conditions is somewhat different. In 1939, German civilians were not called upon to make massive sacrifices for the war effort because, unbeknown to them, they had been doing so for several years already. Under the umbrella of the Four Year Plan, Hitler had been systematically developing the military potential of the German nation since 1936. Huge resources had been taken out of the civilian economy and put into the creation of the necessary infrastructure for a major war effort. There was simply no need for Hitler to take drastic measures to put Germany on a war footing in September 1939, because he had already laid the foundations three

Above: German troops after World War I – "stabbed in the back" according to Nazi myth.

Below: Life goes on as normal – German civilians at a Berlin post office in early 1942.

years earlier. As a result, Germans did not feel the economic pinch of going to war in 1939, because they had already been living in a war economy for three years.

It was also the case that Nazi policy was deliberately geared, as far as possible, towards avoiding unsettling the civilian population. To a large extent this was due to Hitler's belief in the *Dolchstosslegende* (stab-in-the-back theory), the notion that Germany had lost World War I not as a result of military factors, but as a consequence of the collapse of the home front. This was quite untrue. Germany's leaders had called for an armistice in 1918 precisely because their army had been defeated decisively on the battlefield and was in full, if orderly, retreat. This situation was deliberately kept secret

from the German population by the country's generals, who spread the lie that revolution back home, rather than their own failure, had caused the army's collapse. This story was widely believed, not least by Adolf Hitler, who was determined that in the war he unleashed there should be no breakdown in domestic morale. Consequently, with the outbreak of conflict in September 1939, the Nazi regime became extremely sensitive to the popular mood. Aware that emergency war measures could impact negatively on domestic conditions and thereby cause public discontent, the leadership was cautious about introducing such measures and paid close attention to the public reaction when they did so. For instance, when it was discovered that a decree of 4 September 1939 which cut wages and reduced bonuses for weekend, night and holiday work was causing significant discontent, it was rescinded.

Taken together, the result of these factors was that the outbreak of war did not lead immediately to drastic changes in economic and social conditions in Germany. While armaments production rose, there were no real cutbacks in the manufacture of consumer goods such as cosmetics and stockings. Rationing was introduced, but it was set at a generous level and food supplies continued to be plentiful and readily available. Between 1939 and 1941, the calorific content of the food rations available actually increased from 2435 to 2445 calories per consumer. With wages and prices effectively controlled, there was no repeat of the inflationary spiral that had caused so much misery on the German home front in World War I. Instead, people continued to experience the benefits of economic stability. Ironically, there were also some respects in which the war actually made the quality of life better.

Initial military successes by mid-1940, which included the conquests of Poland, Denmark, Norway, the Low Countries and France, provided the Nazi regime with unrestricted access to the labour and raw material resources of these conquered

Above: Issuing ration cards in wartime Nazi Germany. Even with wartime rationing the calorific allowance for each individual German actually increased.

countries. These spoils of war were ruthlessly exploited in order to supply domestic demand in Germany. Occupied Europe was plundered to Germany's advantage.

The fruits of victory

It was not only the vanquished that catered to the needs of the German consumer. Such was the prestige of the German military after the victories of 1940 that most of Europe's neutral states preferred to submit to German demands for "increased economic cooperation". This, in effect, meant supplying the Reich on favourable terms, rather than risking Hitler's displeasure. Imports continued to flow into the Reich in substantial quantities, including iron ore from Sweden, oil from Rumania and grain cereal from the Soviet Union. As with the resources looted from the conquered, these goods worked to limit the impact of the war on people's everyday lives.

While it can be argued that, in the first two years of the conflict, Nazi economic policy ensured that the German public experienced little significant alteration in its standard of living, this claim can easily be overstated. Statistics do not always tell the whole story. While it is true that food rationing did ensure that, at the start of the war, most Germans had access to adequate food supplies, it was still the case that the wartime diet was nutritious but relatively boring. Some staples, such as potatoes, were not initially rationed. Access to popular items, including meat, butter, sugar, eggs and milk, was always severely restricted. Other favourites, such as tea and coffee, were available only in heavily adulterated forms or as *ersatz* (substitute) products. An example was "coffee" made from roasted barley, which one could argue is not really coffee at all. Statistics show that

production of consumer goods remained at near pre-war levels in the first years of the conflict. This does not mean that ordinary Germans were still able to buy these products with the same ease as in peacetime, though. Cars were still manufactured, but were now made exclusively for the *Wehrmacht*, not for civilian consumption. In a similar manner, clothing was still produced in large quantities, but became scarcer as much of the output was used by the military.

Statistical anomalies aside, there were other hidden factors that made life in wartime Germany more arduous than is sometimes suggested. One of these was taxation. War was an expensive business that had to be

Above: German women examining straw shoes for the winter in 1943. By this stage of the war taxes had risen considerably, drastically reducing the purchasing power of ordinary German citizens.

paid for. While the German Government did all it could to shift the burden onto conquered peoples, some of the bill had to be picked up by the German public. Taxes had to rise, and they did so sharply. In addition to the imposition of a war surcharge on income tax, there were also increases in the sales tax, as well as rises on the duties on beer and tobacco. Tax rates effectively doubled during the war, greatly reducing the purchasing power of German citizens, who became unable to afford their pre-war levels of consumption.

While there are grounds for believing that the German population did not experience much hardship in the first two years of the war, there are also reasons for thinking that this picture of a population entirely unaffected by the conflict is an exaggeration. A clear illustration of the relative normality of the first years of the war emerged when, in the winter of 1941, living conditions began to change decidedly for the worse. This change would be so marked that the period 1939–41 would begin to look like a golden age. There were two main reasons for this.

Left: Dr Fritz Todt, the head of construction for the Third Reich's Four Year Plan. He served as Reich Minister for Munitions from 1940, being killed in an air accident in February 1942.

First of all, with the German attack on the Soviet Union on 22 June 1941, the massive losses suffered in the East and the Reich's subsequent declaration of war against America on 11 December of the same year, the *Blitzkrieg* era of easy victories came to an end. This had not been Hitler's intention. Incredible though it may seem, he genuinely expected that Operation Barbarossa, the assault on

Below: As the war on the Eastern Front dragged on, German industry was forced to cast its net wide in its search for workers. Here, elderly men and women receive instructions in an armaments factory.

Russia, would provide him with another speedy triumph. Instead, like former would-be conquerors of Russia such as King Charles XII of Sweden and Napoleon, Hitler found that the vast expanses of Russian territory and the appalling winter weather conditions entirely upset his plans. As his armies stalled in ice, snow and temperatures of 30 degrees below freezing, the prospect of a *Blitzkrieg* victory rapidly evaporated. In its place appeared the unwelcome probability of a long-drawn-out and difficult war of attrition against a determined and powerful adversary. This prospect was multiplied many times over when, six months later, the US was added to the list of Germany's enemies.

This situation forced the Nazi leadership to reconsider its domestic policies. In place of an economic strategy that gave some weight to the needs of the German consumer, it was now self-evidently necessary to introduce one that made the requirements of the armed forces overwhelmingly the number one priority. In the first instance, this meant a massive expansion in armaments production. Some of this increase could be achieved by rationalizing German industry to ensure that it used existing resources better. To this end, a Ministry of Armaments was set up and given the task of removing the inefficiency, waste and duplication of effort that dogged German industrial output. Under the leadership first of Fritz Todt and then, after his death in a plane crash in February 1942, of Albert Speer, it achieved spectacular results. Yet, at the same time, it was also recognized that the desired increase in weapons production could not be achieved without the redirection of at least some industrial facilities and raw materials away from civilian production to the war effort. As a result, this change had

Above: The Allied bombing offensive and the situation in Russia worsened the plight of Germany's civilians. Water supplies were interrupted (left) and individuals had to grow their own vegetables (above).

potentially very serious implications for the quality of life on the home front, a fact that was accepted by the Nazi leadership. As the Führer Order on Armaments of 10 January 1942 observed:

Material and men are increasingly required for the defences in the East. The task of the war economy, therefore, is to produce as large an amount of weapons, munitions and other military equipment as possible and get it to the troops. There is nothing left for civilian production.

Concomitant to this recognition of the need for increased weapons production, there also came an awareness that additional recruitment to the army would be required in order to make good the heavy losses that had been sustained in the bitter battles on the Eastern Front. This, too, had serious implications for life in Germany, as such an expansion in military manpower could be achieved only by transferring out of civilian employment hundreds of thousands of men, whose conscription into the fighting forces had previously been deferred in order to allow them to work in industry. Their sudden departure for the front was not only a considerable blow to their families; it was also a visible indication to the German people that the intensity of the war had increased.

Taken together, the shift to a more vigorous war economy and the redeployment of German workers from the home front to the battle front foreshadowed the end of the relatively comfortable wartime experience that most Germans had so far enjoyed. In some respects the impact of these changes was less marked than might have been expected. The reason was that the Reich was able to find an alternative labour force to replace those who

Below: Albert Speer, Reich Minister for Armaments from 1942. A brilliant administrator, he raised armaments production to high levels. He received a 20-year sentence after the war for his use of slave labour.

were conscripted into the army or were moved to more vital industries.

Unlike in Great Britain, where the departure of male workers to the forces led to the mass mobilization of women in industry, in Germany the new workforce did not consist of female labour. In part, this was because levels of female employment in Germany were already very high. In 1939, for example, 89 percent of single women under 60 were already employed, as were 36 percent of married women. There was no great

reservoir of unemployed female labour in Germany waiting to be tapped. Compounding this, the ideological prejudices of the Nazi leadership against women workers, especially mothers with young children, were too great for them to contemplate the universal conscription of those women who, while capable of work, were not already doing so. While some measures were taken, numerous categories of exemptions acted against the effectiveness of this approach.

Above: A German family surveys what had been their apartment before an Allied bombing raid had reduced it to rubble. At least they had been lucky enough to reach the air-raid shelter before the raid.

Instead, the labour shortage was made up largely by utilizing prisoners of war and foreign slave workers. Even though this substitute labour force was appallingly treated, the sheer numbers of them (there were some seven million conscripted foreign workers in Germany in 1944) ensured that they mitigated at least some of the adverse effects of the redeployment of German workers. However, they could not entirely disguise the fact that conditions had changed. Indeed, things did get significantly tougher for the civilian population. As an example, in the winter of 1944, the average calorific content of the daily food intake sank below the safe minimum of 1800 calories. Additionally, it must be remembered that with fewer German men remaining at home, more families were broken up, and more people's lives altered.

The Allied bombing campaign

Another major reason for the transformation of life inside Germany was the increasing ability of the Allies, by now comprising Great Britain, America and Russia, to bring the war to Germany itself. In place of the "phoney war", the new Allied leadership decided to embark on a "total war" that pitted the full resources of the Allies against the war-making capability of the Third Reich. In practice, this meant the unleashing of a relentless strategic bombing campaign against Germany's cities. With the US Army Air Force (USAAF) conducting operations by day and the Royal Air Force (RAF) operating by night, this campaign brought the full fury of modern warfare to a civilian population that, until 1942, had largely escaped exposure to the destruction and deprivation that the war had unleashed on the rest of Europe. From here on, though, things would be very different.

The enormous impact of the Allied bombing raids on civilian life in Germany reflected their particular nature. Unable, at least at first, to make precision strikes on industrial targets because the bombers were simultaneously too vulnerable to attack in daytime and unable to aim accurately at night, the Allies, particularly the RAF, resorted instead to area bombing. The strategy was to disrupt German war production not by targeting the factories, which were often missed anyway, but by

Above: Cologne cathedral stands comparatively undamaged following a British 1000-bomber raid on the night of 30/31 May 1942. Some 600 acres of the city were destroyed in the raid.

destroying the homes of the workforce in attacks on residential districts. This policy of "de-housing" the German workers, thereby depriving the factories of their supply of labour, was easy to implement. Large urban areas, unlike individual factories, were relatively straightforward to target. Moreover, housing, unlike industrial plant, was less well defended and more easily destroyed. This was a fact that many Germans would soon discover for themselves.

Area bombing

The new area bombing strategy commenced in late March 1942 with a British raid on the coastal city of Lübeck, a target chosen because its narrow streets and half-timbered buildings made it especially vulnerable to attack. This was followed by a series of attacks on other Baltic ports and then by a succession of devastating forays into the interior of Germany, including cities as far south as Munich and Augsburg. However, the main effort was devoted to the industrial cities of the Ruhr valley and, of course, to Berlin. The ferocity of these aerial assaults varied. In 1942, important targets, including industrial cities such as Duisburg, could expect to be hit by 2500 tonnes (2540 tons) of bombs. Lesser targets, such as Nuremberg, might receive only 300 tonnes (305 tons). In a similar fashion, there was considerable variation in the bombing strategy. Some cities were subject to massive individual bombardments. In May

Left: "The day of liberation", a German poster playing on ordinary Germans' fears of the approaching "Red horde". Russian soldiers were dreaded much more than the daily and nightly Allied bombing raids.

Below: In general, morale among Germans did not crumble in the face of Allied bombing. This birthday banner of 20 April 1944 reads: "We greet the first worker of Germany, Adolf Hitler".

1942, for example, 1000 aircraft attacked Cologne in a single night, while Essen experienced a similar 1000-bomber raid some months later. By contrast, other cities were the targets of smaller raids, but were hit more regularly. In a nine-day period in the summer of 1942, Hamburg was attacked no fewer than seven times. Likewise, in the winter months of 1942–43, Berlin endured 16 major night-time raids.

The levelling of Germany

Whatever the exact process, the effects were devastating. In August 1942, British Prime Minister Winston Churchill had told Soviet leader Josef Stalin that "as the war went on, we hoped to shatter almost every dwelling in almost every German city". This was a promise that Air Chief Marshal Sir Arthur Harris, the Head of Bomber Command, made every effort to keep. The attacks he ordered in pursuit of this strategy destroyed nearly 1.8 million homes and forced 5 million people to become refugees. They also knocked out basic amenities for some 20 million people. As an official

report from the Rhineland city of Aachen makes clear, this had a huge impact on everyday life. It described:

the necessity, because of the suspension of public transport, of having to go to work over piles of rubble and through clouds of dust; the impossibility of washing oneself properly or of cooking at home because there was no water, gas or electricity; … the difficulty of shopping for food because most of the shops had been destroyed or had closed of their own accord; the continual explosions of delayed-action bombs or duds or the blowing-up of parts of buildings which were in danger of collapsing; the delay in postal deliveries, the stopping of newspapers; the impossibility of listening to the radio because the electricity had been cut off; the disappearance of every means of relaxation such as the cinema, the theatre, concerts, etc.

Ghastly though these conditions were, it must be remembered that they describe the situation for the "lucky" ones, namely the survivors. The raids also killed 305,000 people and wounded 800,000 more. Many of those who were killed died in

Below: Incendiary bombs fall on Hamburg in July 1943. A German report noted: "The overheated air stormed through the street with immense force … developing in a short time into a fire typhoon."

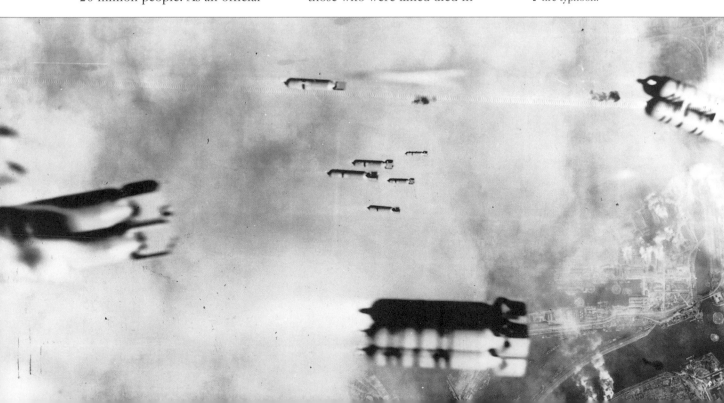

terrifying circumstances. The incendiary attacks on cities such as Dresden created huge firestorms that sucked the oxygen out of the atmosphere, thereby ensuring that many of those who survived the horrors of the intense blast and 1000-degree flames were simply suffocated. The contrast between this kind of experience and the relative calm of the early years of the war could not have been more marked. Albert Speer, being interviewed after the war by Allied officers, remarked of the raids on Hamburg: "We were of the opinion that a rapid repetition of this type of attack upon another six German towns would inevitably cripple the will to sustain armament manufacture and war production. It was I who first verbally reported to the Führer at that time that a continuation of these attacks might bring about a rapid end to the war."

It is by no means clear what effect all this devastation had on the German home front. At one level, there are signs that the effect on domestic morale was quite severe. Certainly, signs of discontent with the regime grew in proportion to the ferocity of the bombing and the level of destruction. This manifested itself first in critical comments about Hermann Göring who, as head of the *Luftwaffe*, was theoretically in charge of air defence. It was then reflected in a more general loss of confidence in the leadership as a whole. One subversive song from the Ruhr that caused particular anxiety to the SD called on the British pilots to "fly on to Berlin; they're the ones who voted Hitler in". There is also some evidence that the raids led to increased absenteeism from the workplace and a growing sense of pessimism and defeatism, a phenomenon that the SD referred to as "air-raid psychosis".

It is also clear that, just as the German Blitz against British cities did not destroy the determination of the British people to persevere in the war, so the Allied bombing of Germany did not cause a sudden collapse in German morale. While not everyone was as calm as Hitler, who casually suggested that the aerial assault against Berlin was simply

clearing the path for his planned rebuilding of the city, the German people did keep fighting until the very end. As Albert Speer, the Minister for Armaments and Munitions, remarked: "The outlook of the people was often poor, but their behaviour was almost excellent." Indeed, there is some evidence that the bombing, far from producing despair, actually increased local solidarity. An example of this steadfastness comes from the diary of Ursula von Kardorff, who confided after a raid on Berlin in January 1944:

I feel a growing sense of vitality within me mixed with defiance, the opposite of resignation. Is that what the English are trying to achieve with their attacks on the civilian population? At any rate, they are not softening us up in the process … if the British think they are going to undermine our morale they are barking up the wrong tree.

In addition, there is plenty of reason to believe that it also produced a strong desire for retribution and revenge, thus possibly increasing people's preparedness to see the war through to the bitter end.

As 1944 rolled into 1945, it was not just Allied planes that German civilians had to worry about. There was also the prospect of invasion by land. In the West, British and American forces had reached the Rhine frontier and were poised to cross into the Ruhr itself. In the East, the Soviet Red Army was on the Vistula, preparing for the final offensive against Berlin. It was clear that Germany itself would soon be a bloody battleground.

This realization, while greeted with grim resignation in the West, was met by fear and consternation in the East. People understood that they faced occupation by the dreaded Russians. Ancient fears of Slavic brutality, combined with the bleak recognition that the indignities and terror meted out to Soviet citizens by German forces in the earlier years of the war would now probably be repaid in full, led to the mass exodus of those able to flee the advancing communist armies. However, the disruption to the transport system made this an arduous and very

Above: US troops and armour cross the Rhine in March 1945. As the war neared its end most German soldiers and civilians alike tried to surrender to British or American forces to save themselves from the Red Army.

dangerous journey. Thousands of civilians died of cold, hunger and exposure in their attempts to escape.

Things were no better for those who chose to remain. There is no doubt that, in seeking revenge, many Soviet soldiers did commit atrocities against German civilians, including theft, rape and murder. Even by the standards of the time, the Soviet invasion of Germany was not a gentle process. The environs of Berlin were soon to be turned into a killing field. The city's commandant, Major General Hellmuth Reymann, calculated that it would take at least 200,000 experienced troops to defend the capital. However, the only ones available to make up the *Volkssturm* (home guard) were mostly old men, women and children. At Hitler's explicit order the city was defended vigorously, a situation that forced the Red Army to fight for every street and every house. In the process, Berlin, a city already battered into oblivion from the air, now faced further destruction from the ground. As tanks and artillery cleared a path

for the advancing infantry, those German civilians unlucky enough to get caught up in the fighting often ended up dead. Fighting was heavy, with house-to-house and hand-to-hand combat. The Soviets sustained an estimated 305,000 dead; the Germans lost as many as 325,000, including civilians.

The situation was no less bleak for the survivors. If the first German experiences of World War II had been of a "phoney war" that took luxury goods out of shop windows and reduced people's disposable income but otherwise barely touched them, then in its concluding years the German populace saw the apocalyptic side of modern warfare. Half of all housing had been destroyed, millions had died or been wounded, and further millions were refugees wandering around Germany trying to reach the Western Allies. To compound this, food was in very short supply and essential services virtually non-existent. Germany was a waste ground; but, then, such was the cost of unleashing World War II.

Above: Troops of the US Seventh Army crossing the Rhine on 26 March 1945. By the beginning of April British and American armies were racing into the heart of Germany itself.

Left: Soviet troops approach the shell-pummelled *Reichstag* during the battle for Berlin, 29 April 1945. After bitter hand-to-hand fighting the building was taken on the 30th, the day Hitler committed suicide.

Below: Soviet troops in the ruins of Berlin, May 1945. On the 2nd General Karl Weidling, the last commander of the city, formally surrendered to the Red Army. The Thousand Year Reich was over.

Chapter 12
Individual lives

Nazism was an ideology that touched the lives of all Germans. For German Jews this meant the gradual erosion of their rights, eventually leading to the concentration camp. However, as this chapter shows, Nazism ultimately adversely affected everyone.

Millions of Germans, men and women, old and young, Nazi and anti-Nazi, cannot reasonably be summarized and categorized without gross distortions. This would only caricature their diversity and complexity. Nevertheless, this chapter attempts to personalize what has been covered more impersonally in the rest of this book. By looking briefly at the lives of four citizens who lived under Nazi rule, a more human dimension is introduced. Each of these people, through their lives, experiences and writings, contributes to deepen our knowledge and understanding of that complex regime. Their shafts of light and enlightenment help to illuminate the darkness of Nazi Germany. It is not being claimed that these four are "typical" Germans (let alone Nazis). Indeed, it

Below: When the Nazis came to power, the lives of German Jews changed for the worse. On 1 April 1933 came the first nationwide action against them: the boycott of Jewish businesses.

is to be hoped that knowledge of their lives and attitudes will make readers question the validity of a concept of a typical "German".

Victor Klemperer

Our first citizen and eyewitness has already been introduced to the reader in Chapter 1, where he was arrested for a breach of blackout regulations. This is Victor Klemperer. Victor was born in 1881 in Prussia, the son of a rabbi. When he married Eva Schlemmer, a musician from a Protestant family, both families were dissatisfied with the match. Victor, despite his academic job, served in a Bavarian artillery regiment on the Western front in 1915–16. This military service, and even more so his "Aryan" wife, were to be crucial in his survival in Nazi Germany, as he relates in detail in the extensive diaries he kept continuously from

1933 to the end of the war in 1945. These diaries, which have entries for nearly every day over the whole life of the Third Reich (as well as a retrospective summary at each year's end), oscillate between the trivial domestic details and the frustrations of a German intellectual who has been thrown out of his job by Nazi anti-Semitic policies, to acute

Above: On the day of the boycott, SA stormtroopers stood menacingly in front of Jewish-owned shops. Signs stated: "The Jews Are Our Misfortune."

193

observations and comments on Nazi rule and the war. Above all, we see in his writings the emergence of Nazi anti-Jewish persecution as observed by a bewildered victim struggling to comprehend what was happening as it happened. As such, there is no comfortable hindsight often found in many memoirs written after the event. Fear, uncertainty and disbelief abound. What is coming next?

The sheer scale and detail of these diaries, which run to more than 1000 pages in their English translation, allow us to reconstruct Victor's life and in part that of his wife, Eva, in great detail. It is often less the events that he describes than his thoughts and reactions to them that are really valuable and insightful. Here, it is possible to give only a sense of that rich detail seen through the eyes of a man whom one English historian reviewer likened to an ordinary suburban resident living in hell. Victor Klemperer frequently expresses his disbelief ("I don't believe it!") and bewilderment at the sheer perversity and stupidity of policies to which he is subjected. We shall focus on one thread that runs inescapably through his life from 1933 to 1945: the experience of anti-Semitism in Germany and particularly Nazi anti-Jewish policy. Victor enables us to see in detail the personal experiences of an individual Jew.

A human dimension

We see the way Victor experiences the initial onset of anti-Semitism from 1933, leading to the "social" death of Jews. The way legislation and grassroots pressure increasingly sets Jews apart from mainstream German society and endangers their jobs. In Victor's case this results in the loss of his university teaching post and his move out of his Dresden apartment to a small house that he and his "Aryan" wife are allowed to

buy. As he reviews his life at the end of 1934 he reminisces about how, in 1897 when he was 16, he learnt to cycle and crashed. Now he wishes at 53 to learn to drive but fears a similar clumsiness will prevent him. "I will have even less presence of mind now than I did then, in addition to a failing heart." This medical reference is another quirky thread through his writings, a sort of hypochondria, at once both irritating and endearingly human. There is his heart palpitations, his headaches, problems with eyesight and his bowels, all of which, as his life progresses, he imagines may be terminal.

Ironically, he displays a toughness, a resilience and a sheer doggedness to keep going (which he will do, although he can't know it) as he deals with the mounting pressures. These include food shortages, worn-out and

Above: The Danzig office of the rabidly anti-Semitic weekly paper *Der Stürmer*. It was run by Julius Streicher, who was sentenced to death by the Allies after World War II. His last words were "Heil Hitler!"

irreplaceable shoes and clothes, desperate cold and fuel shortages in winter, especially in wartime. The long-term effects of all these deprivations on him and his wife as they age and become more frail are recorded. (Incidentally, he did pass his driving test in 1936, only for the Nazis later to deprive Jews of the right to driving licences.)

A loyal wife

The year 1935 and the Nuremberg Laws bring the "civic" death of the Jews. No longer are they full citizens but merely residents in Germany. With the accompanying prohibition on marriages between Aryans and Jews and the general prohibition on sexual relations across "racial lines", this is to Victor and Eva an added crisis. The pressures of the regime were for Aryan partners in existing mixed marriages to divorce their spouses, and arrangements were made to facilitate this. Fortunately for Victor, Eva is loyal and very strong-minded. It is doubtful, despite his own qualities, that Victor would have survived the anti-Semitic policies if the full rigour of those had not in part been deflected by the degree of protection his wife's status and influence, ration books and later ability to move freely, gave him. Just occasionally his own status as an ex-World War I soldier helped, as did a degree of traditional deference to him as *Herr Doktor* or *Herr Professor*! But his wife was really his guardian angel.

The following year, 1936, brought increasing attacks on Jewish property and livelihoods, which were to increase from then on. For Victor this meant persistent battles with the bureaucracy to safeguard his pension and what little he and Eva had in the bank. Petty restrictions and arbitrary changes were the norm, and provide another thread of harassment he had to contend with. His main haven for his own sanity is in reading and research. He is a scholar, although his loss of job at the university means no

Below: Many German Jews were forced to chop firewood to keep themselves warm in winter, as their rights and privileges were stripped away during the 1930s, especially by the 1935 Nuremberg Laws.

library access and the return of all borrowed books. He sets himself permanent goals to continue work on French eighteenth-century culture, working from local libraries and from his own and friends' resources. As the years progress his right as a Jew to borrow library books is removed, and in 1941 his typewriter is impounded. He continues to keep his diary even if it has to be hand-written. He tries to continue his research and begins a new scheme.

Given his interest in languages, he begins to record and comment on Nazi language use. By this he means the deceptions and distortions as language is deformed to disguise the reality of what is being done. This is to form the basis of a book he publishes after the war. Victor's money problems mount with the assessment of Jewish goods and fines which follow the 1938 *Kristallnacht*.

He also takes English lessons as he makes ultimately unsuccessful attempts to leave Germany. His survey for 1938 registers the extent to which his gloomy assessment of 1937 looks positively rosy from the perspective of January 1939. This is a note that is struck again and again.

The increase in fear

The year 1939 brings war, and he and his wife are forced in 1940 out of their little "German" house in the country and into the "Jews" house in Dresden; "too cramped, stuffed full of people". They are now forced into communal living and, as a group, they become more regular targets for bureaucratic harassment: not allowed to use the gardens! Rumours now begin to abound about measures being taken against Jews in Romania and Slovakia – "a ghetto has been set up in the General Government in

Above: A wrecked Jewish shop following *Kristallnacht* in November 1938. To pay for this state-sanctioned destruction, Germany's Jews were collectively fined one billion marks.

Poland and the Jews have been ordered to wear Zion armbands". To this is added news and fears of deportations of Jews from Germany. With the war against Russia, fears increase even more with the introduction of Jewish armbands for German Jews and "at the same time a prohibition on leaving the environs of the city".

From 1941 to 1945 it is a rising nightmare of fear as rumours of murders and massacres on the Eastern Front filter through and deportations of Jews from Germany do begin and increase. More and more of Victor's and Eva's Jewish friends disappear, being sent east. In October 1942 he records: "Both were transported from the women's camp at Mecklenburg to Auschwitz, which appears to be a swift-working slaughterhouse." But still he maintains his secret chronicle while

riven with "fear about my own fate". Yet he and his wife struggle on through the vicissitudes and arbitrariness of Nazi policies as the war continues. Ironically, it is partly the increasing danger from the war

Above: The rise of anti-Semitism: Jews forced to wear the Star of David (top) and anti-Semitic graffiti (above).

that saves them. By early 1945 they are expecting to be deported, but they live in Dresden and in February 1945 the city is destroyed which paradoxically helps to save the Klemperers.

Victor's entries for 13 and 14 February 1945 were written up shortly after the event, but convey with immediacy the drama and danger of those days: the bombs falling in their street, the escape from the damaged shelter, their separation in the immediate confusion and chaos of noise, fires, winds, and his injured and bleeding face as he makes his way to the River Elbe, past the still burning Belvedere and to the Terrace, an area forbidden to Jews. There, sheltering by the Terrace wall he finds his wife. "Eva was sitting unharmed on the suitcase in her fur coat." He reports how his wife acted and observed, whereas he followed his instincts and other people and saw nothing at all. (His wife, a smoker, told him how she nearly lit a cigarette from the only fire source available, a smouldering corpse.) It was "Wednesday 14th of February our lives were saved and we were together".

The journey south

They decide that they should move, little by little, south from Dresden to escape the horror; and Victor, with great fear but ultimately with resolution, removes his star and determines to pass as an Aryan. The danger of the bombs and the fear of the advancing Russians help his resolve. In the chaos he is able to get temporary papers at an office in the small town of Klotzche. Now, "I sit in restaurants, I travel by train and tram – as a Jew in the Third Reich, all of it punishable by death". They move further south into a tiny village where they find shelter and "the food is heavenly": rabbits and milk, pancakes and coffee! They move on

and stay in a pharmacy; fear still haunts them. "My trail as a refugee has been covered" – the growing chaos is too great for any enquiries to be made about him. His diary for 18 March records an unusually lyrical passage as he reflects on his life with his wife and imagines them living on, "Eva and I with angel wings or in some other droll form". The words "impossible" and "unimaginable" have no more validity for him. March moves into April, Victor and Eva move towards Munich and their odyssey continues, for even as the war ends in May they travel back through defeated Germany to Dresden. Klemperer's diary in so many ways reveals that the tragedy of great events is often best revealed through the melodrama of everyday life.

Above: A homeless German woman sorts through what remains of her personal belongings following an Allied air raid. Hitler refused to visit bombed cities to see for himself the heavy destruction.

Christabel Bielenberg may have been seen by readers familiar with the *World at War* series on British television, where she gave brief comments on her experiences of Nazi Germany. For, despite her English background, she married a young German diplomat in 1934 and became a German citizen, which she remained until regaining her British citizenship in 1946. For an English speaking audience she is a particularly interesting observer of Nazi Germany. As she wrote in 1968 when she transferred her diary fragments into book form, in *The Past is Myself*: "I have one advantage, I am English; I was there and above all things German, but above all I was there."

Christabel and her husband Peter returned to live permanently in Germany in late 1935. She was in an optimistic frame of mind, with a handsome husband, a son born in Great Britain and far from hard up. But Hamburg had changed

dramatically in the greater sense of wellbeing and prosperity, and especially in the general feeling that there was a lot to be said for the "New Order". However, the Nuremberg Laws (1935) were part of that new order. When Professor Bauer, a noted paediatrician, had attended her sick child, he politely asked if she would still require his services when the child recovered? For, as a Jew, he was no longer a

Above: Scenes of Dresden following the air raids of February 1945. The Catholic cathedral was ruined (top), and after the raids, which inflicted 70,000 casualties, survivors struggled to return to normality (above).

German citizen and he was warning her of the danger to her through association with him. He later died suddenly, a broken man, probably (his housekeeper was to confide) through suicide.

The *Anschluss* with Austria and the images of violence and anti-Semitic outrages in Vienna led her and Peter to consider emigration, feeling that there was no place for them in the "new" Germany. But while they contemplated their plans, the Czech crisis led to Peter's call-up. Emigration deferred became emigration postponed indefinitely when Peter renewed his acquaintance with Adam von Trott, who convinced him that dissident voices in Germany were re-emerging. They hoped that in the long run this would lead to Hitler's replacement. It is out of this that Peter Bielenberg's association with the 1944 July Plot and conspiracy was to evolve and lead him to a concentration camp.

Wartime Berlin

With the war under way, Christabel was living in Berlin and experiencing for the first time relative poverty, the harsh cold of the winter and the regular reductions in food rations. On a larger scale she was still aware of meetings going on across Germany with von Trott and some army generals and others who still talked of change. But with the defeat of France in 1940, she records finding Winston Churchill's stirring words about fighting on the beaches very unconvincing on the basis of what she had seen in Germany. She has nightmares about Great Britain and her English relatives being beaten into submission. Her recollections reveal so many aspects about Nazi Germany, but only three specific ones will be related here.

The first is from the winter of 1942–43. A friend and neighbour, Ilse, suddenly arrives with a blonde

woman in tow. The woman, she explains, is a Jewess. She and her husband escaped down a fire escape when the *Gestapo* knocked, and have been living in cellars and attics ever since. Christabel is now faced with a moment of decision: "Whether I liked it or not, prepared or unprepared, the moment had come to me." She allows the woman to stay with her that day, but defers a decision about her husband. The fugitive helps with housework all that day. As Peter is away, Christabel consults a trusted friend who accuses her of dangerous folly. On returning to her house the Jewish man is waiting in the shadows for her answer, which is, "only for a night, perhaps two". The couple stay in her cellar. After two days they leave silently in the night. When Christabel recollected the incident for an interviewer for the TV series, she expressed her disappointment with herself and the extent to which the Nazi regime had tainted her humanity.

The 1944 bomb plot

Given the increasingly harsh situation in Berlin, especially the air raids and in consideration of her three children (the third is born in 1942), Christabel is convinced by her husband to move to Rohrbach in the Black Forest. She duly arrives there in September 1943. It is like stepping into another world: the rural remoteness, the strange accents and dialects, and the sense of distance from the war. "Rohrbach was a little world, an unimportant world, which had no say in the affairs of state, but still had to carry the burden of Hitler's dreams of conquest." It is far removed from Berlin, as she discovers when making a brief return visit to the capital where she endures three air raids on three successive nights.

Shortly after that a downed American airman turns up in the

Bavarian forest. Her description of the sheer bewilderment displayed by the local peasants out of a naive interest in this exotic figure borders on the comic. The absence of animosity with which he is questioned, with Christabel acting as interpreter, seems to be more out of curiosity about him and "Colorado" than about his "mission". They reluctantly put him in a cell, and belatedly two local officials from the district authority (not much admired in the village) come to take him away – after which, "the old continued on their way to mass and the able-bodied moved into the fields with their scythes to cut the hay".

These pages:

Scenes of everyday life from Berlin, 1943. Crowding onto public transport to get to work (opposite, top); shoppers go about their business (opposite, bottom); Jews being deported east (above).

201

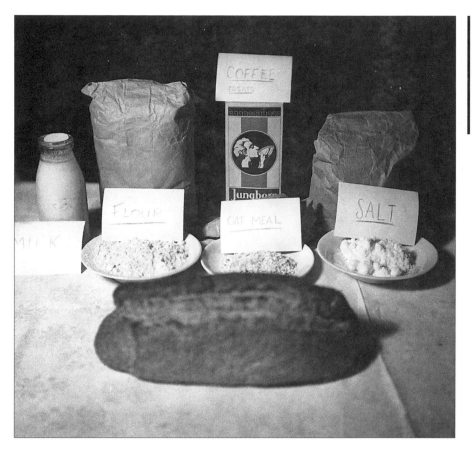

Left: A typical daily ration for a family of four living in Germany in early 1945. The generous rations of the early war years were a distant memory.

Rather more dramatically, one day in July 1944 a neighbour comes rushing in saying, "turn on the wireless, they've thrown a bomb at that Hitler". The news of the failure of the attempt gradually comes through in the ensuing days and weeks, as well as more piecemeal knowledge of arrests. Then a letter addressed to her arrives postmarked Berlin, 25 August 1944. It informs her that Peter was arrested on 6 August. She eventually travels to Berlin to see what help she might be able to give by rousing friends, associates and former colleagues of her husband, anybody who might have influence. When she returns to Rohrbach, the sight of a stranger and a motorbike causes her unease. She is told that the *Gestapo* has asked the mayor to place her under house arrest. His gentle and apologetic explanation suggests it will not be too severe.

Later that winter she is allowed to return to Berlin; a visit has been arranged through contacts for her to see Peter in Ravensbrück. She is given an appointment at 10:00 hours. When her husband is brought into a wooden office to see her, she spots a microphone under the desk. She talks cryptically of a neighbour's four sons who are dead. She hopes he will understand that she means key conspirators, freeing him from the need to protect them. As they shake hands he presses a small matchbox into her palm. This, she learns later, contains snippets of information about the non-political associations with plotters to which he has admitted. As a consequence, she arranges to be interviewed by the *Gestapo* investigator on 4 January 1945 and offers to help with their investigation, now knowing what to say. Lange, the investigator,

Opposite: Typical street scene in Berlin in early 1945. The city had been previously bombed 24 times between 18 November 1943 and March 1944. Each raid had involved up to 1000 aircraft.

203

interviews her as she repeats her totally apolitical approach to everything that has gone on, so that her story coincides exactly with her husband's. Though she feels she has acquitted herself well after her return to Rohrbach, anxiety consumes her until, in the winter of 1945, she records his release and return – two to three days after a phone message had reached the village about his release.

As perhaps her name suggests to an English reader, Mathilde Wolff-Monckeberg was a well-educated, well-connected, well-heeled citizen who came from Hamburg. Having been born in Bismarck's Germany, at the outbreak of World War II she was already 60 years old, with a second husband (who taught at the University of Hamburg). She had six grown-up children, several of whom lived outside Germany, including a daughter, Ruth. In order to maintain some sense of contact with her scattered children, Mathilde began in 1940 to write "letters" for these children that were not posted because of the war and German censorship. She continued this strange one-sided but immensely informative and often moving letter

writing until early 1946. Then Ruth, who was married and lived in Wales, was at last able to visit her mother in post-war Hamburg. Ruth subsequently discovered this substantial cache of letters in her mother's property. She translated them and had them published in 1979 as *On the Other Side*.

They provide a detailed and sustained view of life in war-torn Hamburg from the point of view of a highly literate, cultured, and very redoubtable "lady" who, while a patriotic German, was certainly no Nazi. Mathilde's only outside knowledge came from Nazi newspapers, radio bulletins and hearsay and gossip, so she is not always correct from an historical point of view on some aspects of what she reports. But what she does reveal are her perceptions and fears of what she was actually experiencing in the light of "official" views that she did not necessarily believe, and upon which she often made telling judgements.

She began writing in October 1940 and said she was going to confide to paper "letters that never reached them" so that later her children overseas would know what actually

Below: Collecting for the *Winterhilfe* charity, an organization that raised donations from the better-off to help those Germans less affluent. In 1937, 10 million people received donations.

happened and what things felt like. The harshness of winter in 1940–41 pre-occupies her. She records the severity of 24 degrees of frost with no fuel supplies getting through. But she is occasionally in receipt of letters sent by circuitous routes, mainly via the US or Sweden. The telegram and telephone communications were cut as far as ordinary citizens were concerned. While she comments on her own difficulties, she writes "perhaps you cannot imagine what life is like for Jews". She describes ration cards with a "J" on the outside, confirmation of non-Aryan status; being called Sarah or Israel, required names; never getting special rations for coffee, tea or chocolate; and no clothing coupons. Public notices abound of "Jews not wanted here". She blushes at the vileness and meanness that this engenders, especially as "we others have stood by and said nothing".

As spring advances, she reports the dramatic news of the Western victories and advances of the German armies through Holland, Belgium and France, and she is fearful when she hears, "Now for England". "We hear the 'England song' everywhere. Our parachutists accomplish the impossible and are feared by all our enemies."

Above: War disrupted everyday life in Germany. Food queues added to the general misery (top), while air raids meant taking refuge in an underground shelter (above).

A new and increasingly dominant theme enters her letters: bombing. On 17 May 1941, at 00:30 hours, she describes an air raid, a night she will never forget because of its then unprecedented novelty, the noise, lights and crashing of bombs. She shelters in the air-raid shelter at her block of flats. But it is Harburg nearby, not Hamburg, that is hit. There are 29 dead and 53 wounded and she records: "After this we had to stay in the cellar night after night." The tiredness mounts, schools are closed early for summer. Big events, the continued advances of German troops, are recorded ("the devil has it all his own way") as well as small personal disasters: the loss of her beloved fountain pen and the smashing of her spectacles on the kitchen floor. The visit of a fat policeman to complain about the blackout incenses her, as she not only has curtains but black cardboard stuck over the windows. She realizes there has been a denunciation by a neighbour. "Denunciation is a horrible business" and far too much of it goes on, she comments, even in schools as teachers vet children over their parents' reliability.

Surprisingly, it is not until her entry in January 1942 that she mentions the Russian campaign, when the severity of the cold in Hamburg awakens her sympathy for the endless misery she imagines on the Russian Front, and that of the young widows and despairing mothers, sisters and fiancées she encounters. Her own small, direct anxieties are encompassed in her fights for food, fuel, clothing and shoes. Barter and exchange as in World War I are emerging. She reflects on the appearances of the general population as downtrodden shabbiness, "threadbare coats, shoes down at heel", but despite their cold and misery the majority put up with it all.

She compares herself to elastic being pulled taut by events until it is

Above: The letters of Mathilde Wolff-Monckeberg in this chapter talk of the deterioration in the appearance of the German population during the war, becoming shabby in the face of privations, as here.

overstretched and the spring is gone. May 1942 brings a direct hit by an incendiary bomb. She and her husband are in the shelter when the hellish noise starts and everything begins to shake. She likens it to "somebody emptying a large sack of heavy stones over the house". There is then a blinding flash and the whole street seems to be in flames. Hamburg was being bombed after massive earlier raids on Lübeck and Rostock. Time rolls on remorselessly. She writes: "Yes 1943!", as she describes the curious apathy and dullness of the people; despair, wretchedness, irritation and exasperation on trams, in the post office and in the shops. She compares it with year one of the war when flags were flown at every and any opportunity. Now, "since the capitulation of Stalingrad and the realization of total war, all is grey and still". She is convinced that one cannot believe a word of what the papers say. She sees the changes in herself, comparing her neck to a chicken's gullet and remarks on how she and all others she sees look unhealthy and prematurely aged.

August brings far worse raids over Hamburg, preceded by leaflets that say: "You get a few weeks' respite, then it will be your turn. There is peace now, then it will be eternal peace." This contrasts with the joy another piece of paper brings when a letter from Ruth arrives via a visitor from Stockholm: it is a "draught of joy and strength" which she drinks from. The raids continue, and so much of what she writes is about these: the damage, the danger, the dread. Fears mount in late 1943 of a Russian breakthrough in the East. The fifth winter of the war grows increasingly bleak, and the "bluff and rubbish" in the papers and on the wireless are just so much hollow nonsense for her.

As 1944 advances, the damage and wreckage spreads. Children roam the streets with no schools to go to.

Above: At the end of 1944, with Russian and Allied armies nearing the borders of Germany itself, desperate measures were undertaken to stop them. These labourers are part of the workforce that built barricades in the West.

Thousands spend nights in bunkers. More friends and relatives have moved into her increasingly crowded flat. She describes bartering pieces of furniture for fat and meat. The man from the gas board from whom she hopes to inveigle a new cooker "had to be softened with beer, two sausage sandwiches and finally a cigar". Only her love of music is a partial distraction from the material demands, as she and her husband manage to get to some concerts or listen to the wireless, a welcome diversion from the public loudspeakers. These, she suddenly records on 20 July 1944, reported "that somebody has tried to assassinate the Führer". The whole of Germany is allegedly scandalized by this evil attempt, she adds.

By October 1944 the threat of armies on Germany's frontiers to the west, south and east is recorded, as is Himmler's appeal for a People's Army. But her luck continues as her flat remains relatively comfortable, having escaped so far. An introspective element appears as she (foreseeing or hoping for the war's end) wonders what this period "will look like in memory", as her daily life now seems a series of automatic responses to air-raid warnings and air raids.

At Christmas 1944 her tone is despairing; she quotes a soldier standing behind her at the post office who says it is nothing but "shit and buggery". In January 1945 she compares her sixth winter of the war to what has gone before, which now appears almost light and bright.

Below: As Germany descended into chaos in early 1945, looting became common. These civilians are taking kitchen utensils and blankets from a naval warehouse in Kulmbach. The military have fled.

"We are slowly but surely being strangled." Fugitives from the east roll in. She grows thinner and colder. She counts her few potatoes every day. By April she records the severe punishment Hamburg continues to receive.

On 20 April she talks of the advance of American troops to nearby Harburg, with gunfire rolling across the city. In the queues women talk of the insanity of the situation, of their longing for peace and the resumption of a normal existence. Early May allows her to report that the whole world has changed; part of a crushing nightmare that has oppressed her is now lifted. She listens to English and American broadcasts. "I can go along a road and proclaim loudly, 'Adolf

Above: On 26 April 1945 the Allies captured Bremen. Despite being ringed by heavy anti-aircraft defences, Allied incendiaries and high explosives caused great damage.

Left: A firefighter dampens down flames following an air raid. German civil defence teams were able to do little to alleviate the suffering of the civilian population.

209

Left: This is a typical Third Reich ration card. Without one an individual could not get food. Marianne Strauss, whose story is described on these pages, had no ration card and thus had to beg for food.

Hitler, the most evil criminal in the world', and nobody will tell me to shut up."

Her writing continues until January 1946 but, despite the hardships of another winter, the letters from her family come through and she is at last able to write directly to them.

The Liverpool housewife

A Liverpool housewife who died in 1996 seems an unlikely witness to dramatic and tragic events in Nazi Germany. But her testimony was powerful. Marianne Strauss was born in June 1923 to Jewish parents in Essen; she would survive the Holocaust, unlike her parents and family. From 1943 to 1945 she was on the run, before emerging in Düsseldorf. Her subsequent marriage to a British soldier brought her to post-war Liverpool and an apparently normal life which concealed her tumultuous past. Scant details of this emerged from something she wrote in 1984. But it was not until conversations with Mark Roseman, the historian, and, after her death, the discovery of a collection of letters and diaries, that led Roseman to piece

together a compelling narrative of Marianne's life, which he called *The Past in Hiding*. This biography not only conveyed the particular details of her life, but in dealing with her life on the run revealed the existence of a hitherto unknown underground network which assisted her.

Marianne Strauss and her family were caught up in the unfolding persecution of Jews in Nazi Germany. Despite this, her mother and father, Ine and Siegfried, had made no move to leave by 1938. Then the pogrom of November burst across Germany, and their home town of Essen was no exception. In the aftermath her father and uncle were arrested and sent to Dachau; they were released three weeks later. They then found themselves having to contribute massively to Essen's share of the bill imposed on Germany's Jews by a cynical Hermann Göring to repair the damage of *Kristallnacht*.

It was this crisis that drove the family to seek to emigrate. They joined the complex bureaucratic train to obtain the necessary papers. By August 1939 the process seemed to be nearing completion. The British Consulate in Cologne sent a letter on

17 August and another on 21 August, advising them that their visas were now ready for collection. However, in less than a fortnight Germany and Great Britain were at war. Emigration was now an impossibility.

They continued to try for other possible bolt-holes, but in 1943 they were still in Germany. The records show her father emptying his bank account and selling his remaining assets at four percent of their true value. This all suggests that the family were preparing to leave. When, on 31 August 1943, *Gestapo* agents arrived at Marianne's parents' home, the family were given two hours to prepare to be transported; instead of freedom, they were to be sent east.

This is where we really pick up Marianne's story. While the *Gestapo* were rifling the cellars where the family's belongings were ready for departure, Marianne crept down the stairs and out the front door. Her father had passed her several hundred marks, but she was not able to take any proper leave of her family. She said later that she ran for her life, expecting to hear shots but even that seemed preferable to her imagined and expected fate in the east. "But there was no shot, nobody running after me, no order, no shout." Quite remarkably, *Gestapo* reports of this event survived. The first was a telegram from the Essen *Gestapo* to their supervisors in Düsseldorf:

Left: A German underground air-raid shelter. Many citizens lived a troglodyte existence to escape the bombs.

Below: These are two-roomed wooden houses built for foreign workers. Often located outside towns and cities, they escaped Allied bombs.

Above: Troops of
the 10th Armored
Division, US Third
Army, in the
German town of
Saarburg on 22
February 1945. An
abandoned German
anti-tank gun sits on
the road to the left.

*Re: Evacuation of the Jews Strauss
The Jewess, Marianne Sara Strauss,
born 7.6.1923 resident here. Due to be
taken into custody for the purpose of
evacuation to Theresienstadt, has escaped.*

Two days later, one of the *Gestapo*
agents wrote a fuller report of this
remarkable escape:

*I allowed the Jewess Marianne Sara
Strauss to go to the kitchen ... she then
left the house in an unsupervised
moment. After about five minutes her
absence was noticed.*

Having fled her house, Marianne was
on the run. Amazingly, on 12 August
1943, she had obtained an
international postal ID card for
Marianne Strauss. She omitted the
name "Sara" (obligatory for female
Jews) and was simply noted as
resident in Essen. If her escape was
miraculous, what was to follow is
even more amazing. For, from August
1943 until March 1945 she was to
survive in hiding and on the run in
Nazi Germany. The *Gestapo* in Essen
had assumed she would be recaptured
within three days. How did she
escape detection? Good fortune
played a role, but so did the energy,
fortitude and enterprise of Marianne.
The fact that she was a woman may
have helped. Vitally, an organization
called *Bund* and its courageous
members and associates sheltered and
assisted her.

On escaping from her house she
went to the nearby Blockhaus, an
old wooden school building from
the 1920s. There she cut and
bleached her hair so that people
would not be able to identify her
from the "fugitive" poster that
would shortly appear.

The *Bund* was "the league,
community for social life", an earnest
group of anti-Nazi left-wing
individuals with social consciences.
Marianne had first met them in 1933,
and her involvement continued
thereafter. It was to this group that
she fled in August 1943, where Sonja
Schreiber hid her in the Blockhaus.
Her immediate life of confinement
was to begin. But, ironically, her stay
there was relatively short as Allied
bombing was so intense that the

Opposite: US
troops move through
Cologne in March
1945. The third
largest city in
Germany, by early
March much of it
had been reduced to
rubble. It took the
Allies 57 hours of
street fighting to
capture it.

213

danger to the wooden Blockhaus was too severe. So from October 1943 she began a life on the run, usually with *Bund* members but having to move frequently by train or tram across north and central Germany.

Travelling by trams and trains meant being in a police state without a pass. She had her international postal ID card, but no travel or official papers. She used various stratagems: staying in the toilet; getting off at stations; and moving along trains ahead of pass checkers.

"Outwitting the Nazis"

When she arrived at her destinations, friendly strangers were her only resort – sometimes *Bund* members, occasionally family contacts. Marianne acknowledges the miracle of her survival where there always

seemed a "safety net waiting to catch me", when people risked such dangers to help her out of humanity. How were her "concealers" going to explain her to neighbours, relatives or even their own children, particularly as she seemed fit and healthy and was not working? Moreover, she could not really hide; she had to live relatively openly with her concealers. One ruse was to pretend that she was a young mother with a "borrowed" child. Her hair had been altered again, this time with henna. Ironically, this made her stand out more – she "passed as an Aryan with red hair". Money and food remained a major problem. Coupons were often required, but there were some restaurants that served food without them.

Interviewed in later life about her experiences, she recalled her

Below: German boys play among the debris and ruins with abandoned swords in Wiesbaden, April 1945. Hitler's grandiose Thousand Year Reich, established in January 1933, had lasted 12 years.

determination to "outwit the Nazis ... I pitched my understanding against their stupidity and their bureaucratic rules". Her survival was dependent on the well-organized and courageous commitment of the members of the *Bund*. Marianne also fought intelligently and forcefully for her own survival. She was skilful at producing fabric objects to sell to generate some income. Importantly, as a woman, she had a greater chance than a man who would not have been able to explain why he had neither a job nor a uniform.

The four people discussed in this chapter have been selected partly because they left detailed records. Without records there is no history to be written. In addition, their lives are at one level mundane and undramatic, as their domestic preoccupations often reveal. Nevertheless, they lived in dangerous and dramatic times. The events they experienced and saw cast dark shadows over their country and their lives: the bombing of Hamburg, the persecution of the Jews, the attempted assassination of Hitler, the destruction of Dresden, and the rescue attempts of underground groups – all in various ways touched their lives. Miraculously, all four survived as witnesses – and the texts they wrote will outlast them. They give all of us, and future generations, a view into Nazi Germany, a view "on the other side".

Glossary

Abwehr: German military intelligence organization. After Hitler came to power the *Abwehr* often came into conflict with the Nazi-controlled SD and the *Gestapo*.

Aryan: the name for a prehistoric people who settled in Iran and northern India. From their language, also called Aryan, the Indo-European languages of South Asia are descended. In the nineteenth century the term was used to denote a race responsible for all the progress that mankind had made and who were also morally superior to non-Aryans. The Nordic, or Germanic, peoples came to be regarded as the purest Aryans, an idea seized upon by Hitler and the Nazis.

Aryan Paragraph: Nazi law issued on 11 April 1933 that defined a "non-Aryan": anyone "descended from a non-Aryan, especially Jewish parents or grandparents." A person was considered non-Aryan even if only one parent or grandparent was non-Aryan, especially "if one parent or grandparent was of Jewish faith". All Germans had to prove their Aryan identity with birth certificates, their parents' marriage certificates, and, finally, a detailed genealogical questionnaire. SS officers had to prove their Aryan descent back to 1750. The only person who did not have to fill out this form was Hitler himself.

Auschwitz: Nazi Germany's largest concentration camp and extermination camp, located in southern Poland. Between 1.1 and 1.5 million people were killed at Auschwitz, 90 percent of them Jews.

Autobahnen: German national road network started by the Nazis in 1933. One aim of the programme was to alleviate unemployment, but the roads also appealed to German nationalism and had a strong militaristic intent. About 1000km (600 miles) were completed by 1936, and 6500km (4000 miles) were in use when construction ceased in 1942.

Beer Hall *Putsch*: Hitler's attempt to start an insurrection in Germany against the Weimar Republic on 9 November 1923. The attempted coup in Munich was violently crushed by the police. Hitler subsequently received a five-year jail sentence for treason.

Blitzkrieg: lightning war. A style of warfare used with great success by the *Wehrmacht* between 1939 and 1941. *Blitzkrieg* emphasized the use of speed and shock to disorientate a defender, ultimately resulting in his complete paralysis. Tactics consisted of a breakthrough thrust on a narrow front by combat groups using tanks, dive-bombers and motorized artillery to disrupt the main enemy battle position at the point of attack. Wide sweeps by armoured vehicles followed, creating large pockets of trapped and immobilized enemy forces. Complete aerial superiority ensured that enemy reserves were intercepted before they reached the front.

Blut und Boden: blood and soil. Popular phrase among Nazi speakers that described the mythical relationship between the earth and German peasants.

Bund Deutscher Mädel: League of German Girls. Nazi youth association for girls between the ages of 14 and 18.

concentration camp: internment centre for political prisoners and members of national or minority groups who were confined for reasons of state security, exploitation or punishment. The first inmates of Nazi camps were communists and social democrats, but were quickly followed by Jews, gypsies, homosexuals and anti-Nazi civilians from the occupied territories.

Dachau: the first Nazi concentration camp in Germany, established on 10 March 1933, five weeks after Adolf Hitler became Chancellor. Built at the edge of the town of Dachau, about 16km (12 miles) north of Munich, it became the model and training centre for all other SS-organized camps. Though not an extermination camp, it is estimated that 32,000 died at Dachau from disease and brutality.

DAP: *Deutsche Arbeitsfront*. German Labour Front. The sole labour organization in Nazi Germany. All other organizations, such as trade unions, were made illegal.

Dolchstosslegende: stab-in-the-back theory. The myth that the German Army had not been defeated on the battlefield in World War I, but had been betrayed on the home front. The "stab in the back" legend was used by German right-wing political agitators, especially Hitler, who claimed that Allied propaganda in Germany in the last stages of the war had undermined civilian morale and that traitors among the politicians had been at hand ready to do the Allies' bidding by signing the Armistice.

Einsatzgruppen: SS special action squads. Their task was to murder Jews, Soviet commissars, and gypsies in the areas conquered by the army. Alone or with the help of local police, native anti-Semitic populations and accompanying Axis troops, the *Einsatzgruppen* would enter a town, round up their victims, herd them to the outskirts of the town, and shoot them.

Fascism: a form of right-wing totalitarianism which emphasizes the subordination of the individual to advance the interests of the state. Nazi fascism's ideology included a racial theory which denigrated "non-Aryans", extreme nationalism which called for the unification of all German-speaking peoples, the use of private paramilitary organizations to stifle dissent and terrorize opposition, and the centralization of decision-making by a single leader.

Final Solution: term used by the Nazis to describe the annihilation of European Jewry. The policy was formalized at the Wannsee Conference in January 1942, which was chaired by Reinhard Heydrich and attended by 15 SS and government officials. However, the mass killing of Jews had de facto been undertaken by the Nazis since the beginning of World War II.

Führer: Leader, title used by Adolf Hitler to define his role of absolute authority in Germany's Third Reich. As early as July 1921 he had declared the *Führerprinzip* (Leader Principle) to be the law of the Nazi Party.

Führerprinzip: Leader Principle. In Nazi terms the supreme authority in all things of Adolf Hitler.

Gestapo: *Geheime Staatspolizei*, the Nazi secret state police. The *Gestapo* operated without civil restraints. It had the authority of "preventative arrest", and its actions were not subject to judicial appeal. Before 1939 the *Gestapo* ruthlessly eliminated opposition to the Nazis within Germany. When World War II started, its remit extended into the occupied territories. It was responsible for the roundup of Jews throughout Europe for deportation to extermination camps.

Gleichschaltung: coordination. In a National Socialist sense the process by which the Nazi regime successively established a system of total control and coordination of all aspects of society. The government's desire for total control impelled it to function as the only influence on society. This required the elimination of any other form of influence.

Hitler Jugend: Hitler Youth.

Jungmädelbund: League of Young Girls. Nazi association for girls between the ages of 10 and 14.

KPD: *Kommunistische Partei Deutschlands*. Communist Party of Germany. In the Weimar era the KPD, on orders from Moscow, pursued the fatal policy of concentrating on the social democrats first, knowing that this would lead to a Nazi regime that they believed would soon collapse and be replaced with socialism.

Kraft durch Freude: Strength through Joy. Nazi scheme for the leisure and pleasure of workers. The organization was responsible for the building of two new cruise-liners that were used to take German workers on foreign holidays. The Strength through Joy programme also built sports facilities, paid for theatre visits and financially supported travelling cabaret groups. It also subsidized the development of the People's Car, the *Volkswagen*.

Kripo: *Kriminalpolizei*. Criminal Police. Part of the overall SS organization.

Kristallnacht: Crystal Night, also called Night of Broken Glass. Anti-Jewish pogrom organized in response to the shooting in Paris on 7 November 1938 of the German diplomat Ernst vom Rath by a Polish-Jewish student, Herschel Grynszpan. Just before midnight on 9 November, Gestapo chief Heinrich Müller sent a telegram to all police units informing them that "in shortest order, actions against Jews and especially their synagogues will take place in all of Germany. These are not to be interfered with." Rather, the police were to arrest the victims. In two days and nights, over 1000 synagogues were burned or otherwise damaged. Rioters ransacked and looted about 7000 businesses, killed at least 91 Jews, and vandalized Jewish hospitals, homes, schools and cemeteries.

Lebensraum: living space. A popular political slogan in Germany long before the Nazis came to power. However, Hitler changed the concept from one of acquiring overseas colonies to one of enlarging Germany within Europe itself.

"For it is not in colonial acquisitions that we must see the solution of this problem, but exclusively in the acquisition of a territory for settlement, which will enhance the area of the mother country, and hence not only keep the new settlers in the most intimate community with the land of their origin, but secure for the total area those advantages which lie in its unified magnitude." (Hitler, *Mein Kampf*)

Luftwaffe: German Air Force.

Mein Kampf: *My Struggle*. Political manifesto written by Adolf Hitler. The first volume, entitled *Die Abrechnung* ("The Settlement [of Accounts]", or "Revenge"), was written in 1924 in Landsberg, where Hitler was imprisoned after the abortive Beer Hall *Putsch* of 1923. It covers the world of Hitler's youth, World War I and the "betrayal" of Germany's collapse in 1918. It also expresses Hitler's racist ideology, identifying the Aryan as the "genius" race and the Jew as the "parasite", and declares the need for Germans to seek living space (*Lebensraum*) in the East at the expense of the Slavs and the hated Marxists of Russia. It also calls for revenge against France. The second volume, entitled *Die Nationalsozialistische Bewegung* ("The National Socialist Movement"), written after Hitler's release from prison in December 1924, outlines the political programme, including terrorist methods, that National Socialism must pursue both in gaining power and in exercising it thereafter in the new Germany.

National Socialism: political ideology of the Nazi Party. The two concepts of "national" and "social" had been fashionable in Germany before 1914. The Nazis took these ideas a step further, building a political movement upon two core principles: anti-Semitism and pan-Germanism. Interwoven around these ideas were the myth of blood and soil, the "master race" idea, and the utopian vision of Germany conquering *Lebensraum* in the East and "Germanizing" the conquered area.

Nazism: the totalitarian fascist ideology and policies espoused and practised by Adolf Hitler and his Nazi Party. Nazism stressed the superiority of the Aryan, its destiny as the "master race" to rule the world over other races, and a violent hatred of Jews, which it blamed for all of Germany's problems. Nazism also provided for extreme nationalism which called for the unification of all German-speaking peoples into a single empire. The economy envisioned for the state was a form of corporative state socialism, although members of the party who were leftists (and would generally support such an economic system over private enterprise) were purged from the party in 1934.

Nietzsche, Friedrich (1844–1900): German philosopher and poet best known for *Thus Spoke Zarathustra*. He theorized that there were two moral codes: that of the ruling class (master morality) and that of the oppressed class (slave morality). The ancient empires grew out of a master morality, and the religions of the day out of the slave morality (which denigrated the rich and powerful, rationalism and sexuality). He developed the concept of the "overman" (superman) which symbolized man at his most creative and highest intellectual capacity. His writings had a major influence on Nazi ideology.

Night of the Long Knives: purge of the SA on 30 June 1934. The SA was regarded with suspicion by the regular army and by wealthy industrialists, two groups whose support Hitler was trying to secure. Despite Hitler becoming Chancellor in January 1933, Ernst Röhm, the leader of the SA, continued to agitate for a "second Nazi revolution" of a socialist character, and he hoped to merge the regular army with the SA under his own leadership. Therefore, using the SS, Hitler liquidated the SA leadership, including Röhm.

NSDAP: *Nationalsozialistische Deutsche Arbeiterpartei*. The National Socialist German Workers' Party.

Nuremberg Laws: a series of anti-Jewish laws first made public at the 1935 Nuremberg Rally and enforced from September of that year. Under the new laws Jews could no longer be citizens of Germany. It was also made illegal for Jews to marry Aryans.

OKW: *Oberkommando der Wehrmacht*. German Armed Forces High Command.

People's Court: Nazi special criminal court. First established in 1934 to ensure that cases with political ramifications would be dealt with acceptably and in conformity with party principles.

Reichstag: building in Berlin that was the meeting place of Germany's national legislature. A neo-Renaissance building, it was gutted by fire in February 1933.

Reichstag fire: the burning of the *Reichstag* (parliament) building in Berlin on the night of 27 February 1933. This was a key event in the establishment of the Nazi dictatorship and was widely believed to have been contrived by the newly formed Nazi government itself, to turn public opinion against its opponents and to assume emergency powers.

RSHA: *Reichssicherheitshauptamt*. Reich Security Head Office. The central SS department which controlled all official and secret police and security organs of the Third Reich. There was a multitude of departments, offices, groups and sub-divisions.

SA: *Sturmabteilung*. Storm Detachment or stormtroopers, also called Brownshirts. A paramilitary Nazi organization whose methods of violent intimidation played a key role in Adolf Hitler's rise to power. Founded in Munich by Hitler in 1921 from the *Freikorps* (Free Corps), which were groups made up of ex-soldiers who battled leftists in the streets. They dressed in brown uniforms following the fashion of Mussolini's fascist Blackshirts in Italy.

SD: *Sicherheitsdienst*. Security Service. A Nazi security department in charge of foreign and domestic intelligence and espionage. In 1939 the SD was joined with the *Sipo* to form the *Reichssicherheitshauptamt* (Reich Security Head Office) under Heydrich.

SPD: *Sozialdemokratische Partei Deutschlands*. Social Democratic Party of Germany. The largest political party in the Weimar Republic until 1932, when the Nazi Party overtook it. The SDP voted against the Enabling Act in March 1933, which gave Adolf Hitler dictatorial powers. The Nazi Party banned the SDP in June 1933, and subsequently most of its leaders were arrested and sent to concentration camps.

SS: *Schutz Staffel*. Protection Division. The black-uniformed élite corps of the Nazi Party. Founded by Adolf Hitler in April 1925 as a small personal bodyguard to protect him at public meetings, the SS grew with the success of the Nazi movement. Headed by Heinrich Himmler from 1929 until 1945, entry into the SS was governed by strict racial criteria. By 1939 the black guard numbered 250,000 men, divided mainly into two groups: the *Allgemeine-SS* (General SS) and the *Waffen-SS* (Armed SS). By the end of World War II the *Waffen-SS* numbered over one million men.

swastika: symbol of the Nazi Party and Third Reich. Originally an ancient symbol, until the Nazis adopted it the swastika was used by many cultures throughout the world to represent life, sun, power, strength and good luck. The Nazi flag was a black swastika upon a white circular background, with a red surround. "In red we see the social idea of the movement, in white the nationalistic idea, in the swastika the mission of the struggle for the victory of the Aryan man, and, by the same token, the victory of the idea of creative work, which as such always has been and always will be anti-Semitic." (Hitler, *Mein Kampf*)

Third Reich: official Nazi designation for the regime in Germany from January 1933 to May 1945, as the presumed successor of the medieval and early modern Holy Roman Empire of 800 to 1806 (the First Reich), and the German Empire from 1871 to 1918 (the Second Reich).

Thousand Year Reich: another name for the Third Reich. Hitler endeavoured to align his movement with great successes of the past that would resonate within the German people, and he definitely intended that his creation would bring his name and image to the whole world for 1000 years, so both terms were used repeatedly to build this sense of history, strength and inevitability in the minds of all Germans.

Treaty of Versailles: peace document signed at the end of World War I by the Allied and Associated Powers and by Germany in the Hall of Mirrors in the Palace of Versailles, France, on 28 June 1919. It took effect on 10 January 1920. There were many clauses in the treaty that would later aid the Nazi rise to power. For example, the population and territory of Germany was reduced by about 10 percent. In addition, the "war guilt clause" of the treaty deemed Germany the aggressor in the war and consequently made her responsible for making reparations to the Allied nations in payment for the losses and damage they had sustained in the war. In a move that enraged nationalists, the German Army was restricted to 100,000 men; the general staff was eliminated; and the manufacture of armoured cars, tanks, submarines, airplanes and poison gas was forbidden.

volkisch: of the people. In Nazi terms a phrase associated with anti-Semitism and extreme nationalism. During the late nineteenth century Germany experienced a growth in what was termed *volkisch* beliefs. A raft of small groups, clubs and lodges sprang up espousing differing versions of the same basic set of ideas. Some of these beliefs included racial purity, fitness of body and mind, the sanctity of the land, patriotism and loyalty to family. One of the more prominent groups, the *Germanenorden*, split and reformed in 1918 into the *Thule Gesellschaft*. Members of the *Thule* included Rudolf Hess, publisher Anton

Drexler and a young Adolf Hitler. In time the members of the *Thule* formed the core of the emergent National Socialist Party.

Völkischer Beobachter: *People's Observer*, a daily newspaper. Bought by the Nazis in 1923, it was essentially a propaganda organ of the Nazi Party.

Volksgemeinschaft: People's Community. In National Socialist terms this meant individuals were subservient to the totalitarian state. The interests of the state came before the interests of the individual, and blind obedience to the *Führer* was encouraged. In addition, some groups, notably "inferior races", were excluded from the people's community.

Volkssturm: German People's Militia. Constituted in September 1944. The organization may be considered a territorial militia which was formed and called to arms only for training purposes or for employment whenever a local area was threatened by the enemy. Men between the ages of 16 and 60 were recruited into the *Volkssturm*, many without uniforms or weapons. *Volkssturm* units were widely used in 1945.

Wall Street crash: American economic disaster in October 1929, when prices on the stock market in the United States collapsed completely. In Germany American investors, anxious about their financial position, began withdrawing their loans. German indebtedness to these investors had by 1929 reached nearly 15 billion marks. Prices on the German stock exchange fell, business failures multiplied, and unemployment rose to three million during the course of the year. By the winter of 1932 it had reached six million. The crash aided the Nazis, whose extreme policies suddenly became attractive to Germans desperate to preserve their living standards.

Weimar Republic: the name given to the German government between 1919 and 1933. In February 1919, following defeat in World War I, a national assembly met in Weimar, 240km (150 miles) southwest of Berlin, because the capital was not safe due to internal unrest. A signature of the hated Versailles Treaty, Weimar was detested by both nationalists and right- and left-wing politicians alike.

Weltanschauung: world view. One of Hitler's favourite terms, and one used by him to elevate any trivial opinion or viewpoint into an ideological concept.

Zyklon B: a commercial form of hydrocyanic acid, which becomes active on contact with air. It was manufactured by a firm called Degesch, which was largely owned by I.G. Farben, and it had been brought to Auschwitz in the summer of 1941 as a vermin-killer and disinfectant. It was used to murder victims in the gas chambers of Auschwitz.

Bibliography

Barkai, Avraham, *Nazi Economics: Ideology, Theory, and Policy*, Yale: Yale University Press, 1990

Bartov, Omer, *The Eastern Front 1941–45: German troops and the barbarisation of warfare*, London: Macmillan, 1985

Bartov, Omer, *Hitler's Army: Soldiers, Nazis, and War in the Third Reich*, New York & Oxford: Oxford University Press, 1992

Bielenberg, Christabel, *The Past is Myself*, London: Corgi, 1968

Bridenthal, Renate, *When Biology Became Destiny: Women in Weimar and Nazi Germany*, New York: Monthly Review Press, 1984

Browning, Christopher R., *Ordinary men: Reserve Police Battalion 101 and the Final Solution in Poland*, New York: HarperCollins, 1992

Buchheim, Hans, *Anatomy of the SS State*, London: Collins, 1968

Bullock, Alan, *Hitler: A Study in Tyranny*, London: Penguin Books, 1964

Burleigh, Michael, *The Third Reich: A New History*, Basingstoke: Macmillan, 2000

Cooper, Matthew, *The German Army 1933–1945: Its Political and Military Failure*, London: Macdonald and Jane's Publishers, 1978

Cornwell, John, *Hitler's Pope: The Secret History of Pius XII*, London: Penguin, 2000

Cracauer, Siegfried, *From Caligari to Hitler: A Psychological History of the German Film Industry*, Princeton: Princeton University Press, 1966

Cross, Robin, *Fallen Eagle: The Last Days of the Third Reich*, London: Caxton, 2000

Engel, David, *The Holocaust: The Third Reich and the Jews*, Harlow: Longman, 2000

Fest, Joachim, *The Face of the Third Reich: Portraits of the Nazi Leadership*, London: Penguin, 1972

Fleming, Gerald, *Hitler and the Final Solution*, Berkeley: University of California Press, 1987

Gellately, Robert, *Backing Hitler: Consent and Coercion in Nazi Germany*, Oxford: Oxford Paperbacks, 2002

Gilbert, Martin, *Atlas of the Holocaust*, London: Michael Joseph, 1982

Gilbert, Martin, *Final Journey: The Fate of the Jews in Nazi Europe*, London: George Allen and Unwin, 1979

Grunberger, Richard, *A Social History of the Third Reich*, Harmondsworth: Penguin, 1974

Haffner, Sebastian, *The Meaning of Hitler: Hitler's Use of Power. His Successes and Failures*, New York: Macmillan, 1979

Haigh, R.H., *The Rise and Rise of the Third Reich: Nazi Foreign Policy 1933–1939*, Sheffield: Sheffield Hallam University, 2001

Hilberg, Raul, *The Destruction of the European Jews*, London: Yale University Press, 2003

Hitler, Adolf, *Mein Kampf*, London: Hutchinson, 1976

Holborn, Hajo, *Republic to Reich: The Making of the Nazi Revolution*, New York: Vintage, 1973

Hull, David Stewart, *Film in the Third Reich: A Study of the German Cinema 1933–1945*, Berkeley: University of California Press, 1969

Kershaw, Ian, *The Nazi Dictatorship*, London: Edward Arnold, 1985

Kershaw, Ian, *Popular Opinion and Political Dissent in the Third Reich: Bavaria 1933–1945*, Oxford: Clarendon, 1983

Kershaw, Ian, *Hitler 1936–1945*, London: Penguin Books, 2001

Kershaw, Ian, *Hitler 1889–1936*, London: Penguin Books, 2001

Klemperer, Victor, *I Shall Bear Witness: the Diaries of Victor Klemperer, 1933–41*, London: Phoenix Press, 1999

Klemperer, Victor, *To The Bitter End: the Diaries of Victor Klemperer 1942–45*, London: Phoenix Press, 1999

Layton, Geoff, *Germany: The Third Reich, 1933–45*, London: Hodder & Stoughton, 2000

Lucas, James Sidney, *Last Days of the Reich: The Collapse of Nazi Germany, May 1945*, London: Cassell, 2001

Maser, Werner, *Hitler: Legend, Myth and Reality*, New York: Harper and Row, 1973

McDonough, Frank, *Opposition and Resistance in Nazi Germany*, Cambridge: Cambridge University Press, 2001

Meyer, Henry Cord, *The Long Generation: Germany from Empire to Ruin, 1913–1945*, New York: Harper Torchbook, 1973

Milward, Alan S., *The German Economy at War*, London: The Athlon Press, 1965

Müller, Klaus-Jürgen, *The Army, Politics and Society in Germany 1933–45: Studies in the Army's relation to Nazism*, Manchester: Manchester University Press, 1987

Noakes, Jeremy (ed.), *Nazism 1919–1945, Volume 4: The German Home Front in World War II*, Exeter: University of Exeter Press, 1998

Noakes, Jeremy & Pridham, Geoffrey, *Documents on Nazism, 1919–1945*, London: Jonathan Cape, 1974

O'Neill, Robert J., *The German Army and the Nazi Party, 1933–1939*, London: Cassell & Company, 1966

Overy, R.J., *War and Economy in the Third Reich*, Oxford: Clarendon Press, 1994

Peukert, Detlev J.K., *Inside Nazi Germany: Conformity, Opposition and Racism in Everyday Life*, London: Penguin Books, 1989

Reitlinger, Gerald, *The Final Solution: The Attempt to Exterminate the Jews of Europe*, London: Sphere, 1971

Reitlinger, Gerald, *SS: Alibi of a Nation*, London: Arms & Armour Press, 1981

Rentschler, Eric, *The Ministry of Illusion: Nazi Cinema and its Afterlife*, Cambridge, MA: Harvard University Press, 1996

Rich, Norman, *Hitler's War Aims: Ideology, the Nazi State, and the Course of Expansion*, New York: W.W. Norton, 1973

Röhl, J.C.G., *From Bismarck to Hitler: The Problem of Continuity*, London: Longman, 1970

Roseman, Mark, *The Past in Hiding*, London: Penguin Books, 2001

Rosenbaum, Ron, *Explaining Hitler: The Search for the Origins of his Evil*, London: Papermac, 1999

Schoenbaum, David, *Hitler's Social Revolution: Class and Status in Nazi Germany 1933–1939*, New York: Anchor, 1966

Schweitzer, Arthur, *Big Business in the Third Reich*, Indiana: Indiana University Press, 1977

Smith, Woodruff D., *The Ideologiocal Origins of Nazi Imperialism*, Oxford: Oxford University Press, 1989

Speer, Albert, *Inside the Third Reich*, London: Phoenix, 1995

Stachura, Peter, *The Shaping of the Nazi State*, London: Croom Helm, 1978

Steinhoff, Johannes, Pechel, Peter & Showalter, Dennis (eds.), *Voices from the Third Reich: An Oral History*, London: Grafton Books, 1991

Stephenson, Jill, *Women in Nazi Germany*, London: Croom Helm, 1975

Stone, Norman, *Hitler*, London: Hodder and Stoughton, 1989

Toland, John, *Adolf Hitler*, New York: Doubleday, 1976

Townley, Edward, *Hitler and the Road to War*, London: Collins Educational, 1998

Welch, David, *The Third Reich: Politics and Propaganda*, London & New York: Routledge, 1995

Welch, David, *The Hitler Conspiracies: Secrets and Lies Behind the Rise and Fall of the Nazi Party*, Shepperton: Ian Allan, 2001

Wolff-Monckeberg, Mathilde, *On the Other Side*, London: Pan, 1979

Index